TABLE OF CONTENTS

"AI killed me"

Imagine this: an artificial intelligence capable of generating ten thousand scientific hypotheses overnight, then running its own simulations to determine which ones work. What human science would have taken a century to explore becomes an instant reality. Medicine, physics, and biology leap forward by a thousand steps at once. Humanity wakes up in a world where it no longer understands the discoveries made the day before.

That same vertigo has now reached commerce—the field that once believed it had already secured its digital future. But the truth is simple: e-commerce is already dead. It has not been replaced by a rival platform, but by an intelligence that no longer needs it.

If there were a message left on the wall of the digital crime scene, it would read: "AI killed me." Like Frankenstein's creature, e-commerce built its own killer. It identified its executioner, empowered it, and handed over the tools of its own extinction.

E-commerce has committed economic suicide. The proof is everywhere. Customer acquisition costs have exploded across every major platform—Google, Meta, Amazon, TikTok. What once cost a few cents now costs tens of euros per customer. Margins are collapsing, and smaller players are disappearing. The model has devoured itself in an endless bidding war that only enriches the platforms controlling the flow of attention.

Step by step, e-commerce engineered its downfall. It surrendered control to the digital giants—Google, Facebook, Amazon—believing their ecosystems would ensure survival. They owned the traffic, the data, the pricing, and now, the algorithms. E-commerce entrusted its destiny to them, and those hands now belong entirely to artificial intelligence.

It then produced an ocean of behavioral data that became AI's raw material. Every click, every purchase, every abandoned cart helped train the predictive systems that now render it obsolete. For a quarter of a century, e-commerce built the very data infrastructure that has made it unnecessary.

It conditioned consumers to expect immediacy and prediction— delivery in twenty-four hours, then two, then one; extreme personalization; algorithmic recommendations. The consumer no longer wants to search. He wants to receive. And AI can deliver that with surgical precision.

Finally, e-commerce buried itself under its own complexity. Too many products, too many options, too many steps. The customer no longer wants to decide; he wants decisions made for him. Artificial intelligence fulfills that wish effortlessly.

The outcome is inevitable. Every attempt to strengthen the model has only accelerated its demise. E-commerce designed the perfect crime against itself. The message remains engraved in the code of the digital age: "AI killed me."

Signed: E-commerce.

PRÉFACE

AI will not replace e-commerce. It will absorb it.

There will be a before, and there will be an after.
Artificial intelligence is not just another innovation. It is not a tool. It is not a technological gadget that you plug into a marketing strategy the way you activate a new feature on Shopify. AI is a fracture. A rupture. An entity.
It is the greatest human invention of all time—and it will also be the last. Because the next ones, the ones that will transform our industries, our habits, and our mindsets, will either be created by it or made possible through it. We have just handed over the torch of innovation.

In the world of e-commerce, that changes everything. Absolutely everything.
Those who still believe that AI will "boost their sales" or "optimize their campaigns" have understood nothing.
What artificial intelligence is doing is not improving the rules of the game; it is destroying the playing field, redrawing it, and rewriting its laws, behaviors, and power structures.
Digital marketing will not be enhanced. It will be digested—and then surpassed.

I remember perfectly the early days of the Internet and of e-commerce.
It was the late 1990s, the dawn of the 2000s. I founded HairStore in that context.
I was young, determined—perhaps a little reckless—but convinced that the future of commerce would unfold on a screen.
People looked at me as if I were delusional. Doors closed in my face. I can still see that banker, smiling faintly, telling me, "No one will ever buy shampoo on the Internet."

Two decades later, I watched the skeptics disappear and certainties melt away.
And today, I see the same blindness toward artificial intelligence.
The same condescension. The same inertia.

But this time, evolution will not take twenty years. It will take three. Perhaps two. Perhaps less...

This book is not a complaint. It is not a panicked manifesto.
It is a calm alarm bell placed on the digital counter of a generation of entrepreneurs. I

do not believe that AI is a threat. I believe it is a historic opportunity. But we must understand it. We must look it in the eye. We must prepare for it—now.

What I call AI-Commerce is the post-e-commerce era. It is the moment, already underway, when companies that grasp the logic of predictive models, autonomous architectures, and frictionless experiences will win.
The others will watch. And then they will fade.

I wrote this book as one draws a topographic map of a still-unstable continent.
But I do not rely only on intuition or observation; I also build on my own doctoral research on the automation of marketing and artificial intelligence, at the intersection of technology, strategy, and human behavior.

I wrote it so that we can stop believing AI will help e-commerce or digital marketing. It will not help them. It will replace them.

And you can choose to be part of it—or to stand aside and watch the wave pass.
But do not say, tomorrow, that no one warned you.

Marco-Paulo DA CRUZ
PhD in Digital Marketing Science
Founder of HairStore.fr

Chapter 1 – The Mirage of Modern Ecommerce

Introduction

For a long time, ecommerce was seen as a promised land—a horizon of freedom, growth, effortless automation, and passive income. A place where customers would flow in day and night while the merchant slept. A smooth world, predictable, accessible to anyone with ambition and a Wi-Fi connection. This myth shaped an entire generation of entrepreneurs—and I know it well, because I came from it.

But today, the mirage is fracturing. Slowly at first, then violently. Behind the glitter of growth charts and market reports, customer acquisition costs are exploding, margins are evaporating, and differentiation is becoming an illusion. And above all, the rules are changing. Not because of a new competitor or a new channel, but because of a systemic entity that rewrites the very logic of commerce itself: artificial intelligence.

This chapter is a scalpel against the façade. It dissects, piece by piece, the illusions still clinging to what people call "modern" ecommerce. I say "modern" with irony—because what most actors consider modern today is already obsolete. We are still selling like it's 2010 and thinking like it's 2005. The websites have evolved, the interfaces are slicker, the CMS smoother—but the underlying logic remains the same: a product, a storefront, a funnel, a click. This model is not endangered; it is outdated.

Yet the ecosystem keeps investing in obsolete mechanics, as if fitting new tires on a car destined for the scrapyard. Why? Because ecommerce has become a religion. And like every religion, it survives not on evidence, but on belief.

1.1 – The Shopify–Amazon Model: Temple or Illusion?

For more than a decade, two names have embodied the myth of the digital Eldorado: Shopify and Amazon. Two pillars, two symbols. One promised absolute independence; the other offered immediate audience. On one side, the free entrepreneur, sovereign and self-reliant. On the other, the most powerful commercial engine ever built. Together, they defined the mental architecture of modern ecommerce.

But this model is a trap—a comfortable, seductive, reassuring trap. A technological trap, an economic trap, a cognitive trap. Shopify and Amazon are not temples of modern commerce. They are simulators. Sophisticated interfaces built on a paradigm that is already collapsing: the belief that humans decide, click, and buy, and that merchants control.

Take Shopify. It is sold as the ideal gateway for any business that wants to "go digital." Easy to use, packed with extensions, and compatible with all marketing tools. On paper, a promise of sovereignty. In reality, a gilded cage. Most Shopify stores do not survive three years. The reasons are structural: advertising costs have exploded, competition is global, and visibility has become an algorithmic privilege. Having a store is no longer enough. The illusion of control that Shopify offers hides the real dependency—on Meta, Google, TikTok, on slashed prices, on tired dropshipping tactics, on the "10% off your first order" coupons that everyone uses and no one notices.

Shopify's problem is not technical. Its technology is strong. Its problem is strategic: it does not capture intent—it waits for it.

Shopify is a passive tool in a world becoming aggressively proactive. The new era is one of AI assistants, intent engines, and invisible triggers. Within that logic, Shopify is misaligned. It does not sell traffic. It does not detect demand. It does not preempt behavior. It welcomes. But welcoming no longer works.

Amazon, on the other hand, represents the extreme of the opposite logic. Here, the entrepreneur surrenders everything. The brand becomes a SKU. The strategy becomes a text field. The margin becomes a variable in the Buy Box algorithm. Amazon delivers sales—but at the cost of vision, autonomy, and relationship. It is a hydra: it gives performance and devours identity.

The trap here too is structural. Amazon operates on a hyper-logistical, hyper-industrialized model, where differentiation is sacrificed for speed. The product is king—but the product no longer sells. What sells now is the fine detection of intent, upstream of the act. And in that new battle, Amazon is growing blind. Its brute power—its catalog, its supply chain, its Prime ecosystem—is no longer enough. Because the war is no longer about the offer—it is about the algorithmic orchestration of desire.

Two trajectories emerge.
 On one side, Shopify, once a tool of sovereignty, now unsustainable without massive paid traffic, must evolve into an AI-native platform. That means ceasing to be a CMS and becoming a predictive orchestration engine. Anticipating intent, scripting journeys, piloting hyper-personalized recommendations. It means abandoning the idea of the "store" and becoming an invisible, conversational, contextual layer.

On the other side, Amazon, the centralized fortress turned battlefield of price, faces a choice: concentration or implosion. It must either embrace the personal assistant era—through Alexa, through the connected home, through predictive subscriptions—or rctreat into logistics and let others own the customer relationship. But it cannot remain what it is now: an overloaded interface in a world fleeing interfaces.

Yet both models are still taught as gospel. They remain checkbox references in business plans, benchmarks in entrepreneurship courses, examples in every "ecommerce success" webinar. Meanwhile, reality says something else: Shopify creates micro-merchants dependent on paid traffic. Amazon manufactures interchangeable executors in an opaque ecosystem. And now AI is closing the trap—automating even the act of purchase itself.

The truth is, these platforms are not the future. They are the extension of a past that refuses to die. Their logic is linear, but consumers are not. They do not wait. They do not choose. They are anticipated—or rather, anticipation is done for them. The real power no longer lies in "who has the best offer," but in "who knows you will buy before you do."

Shopify and Amazon are not enemies to destroy—but idols to dethrone. They are not models, but static structures unable to absorb what's coming: purchases without interfaces, decisions made by personal AIs, journeys managed entirely by conversational algorithms. They are too heavy, too product-centered, too funnel-bound.

In the near future, the platforms that survive will be those that no longer need to be seen— invisible, intelligent, integrated into the environment. They will not be marketplaces. They will be ecosystems of intent.

Shopify and Amazon are dinosaurs. Impressive, massive—but cold-blooded in a world that's turning into a storm.

1.2 – The Augmented Customer No Longer Buys: He Is Bought

For decades, the customer was the alpha and omega of every commercial strategy. He was the one to seduce, attract, and convince. The "purchase act" was treated as something deliberate, thoughtful, almost sacred. The entire discipline of marketing rested on a fiction: that the customer chooses.

That is no longer true.

Today's customer is saturated, fragmented, assisted, and guided. He no longer buys autonomously—he is bought. Bought by the algorithm that pushes him, by the notification that draws him in, by the prediction that anticipates his behavior better than he himself can. This is not a metaphor but an anthropological shift.

Artificial intelligence has rewritten the commercial equation. We no longer live in a world of supply and demand but in a world of preempted intent. AI does not wait for you to express a need—it infers it, shapes it, and stages it.

Consider a simple example: recommendation platforms. What Netflix did for series, Amazon does for razors. But the process no longer stops at recommendation. AI triggers. AI executes. It pushes the logic of "one-click" to its final destination: zero-click.

Tomorrow, you will no longer order your detergent. It will arrive. Your voice assistant will have cross-referenced your laundry frequency, your habits, your purchase history, and your calendar. The need will be met before it is felt. The line will have been crossed. Intention will no longer be human.

The augmented customer is not freer. He is more controlled, more assisted, more predictable. He becomes a probabilistic profile—a series of anticipated actions, a statistical portrait optimized for conversion. That profile is the real product. The customer no longer chooses the product. The product chooses the customer.

Behind this inversion lies a precise and relentless mechanism: algorithmic nudging. Invisible micro-incentives shaping decisions without awareness. A color, a phrase, a moment, a missing click—each element engineered to provoke action without deliberation.

In this world, traditional marketing looks absurd. A ritual dance in an empty room. You speak to someone who has already been persuaded elsewhere—by a machine faster, subtler, and infinitely more patient than you.

This is the wall that traditional ecommerce hits: it still believes in the act of purchase. It invests in tunnels, carousels, retargeting campaigns, while the act of purchase itself is becoming an exception rather than the norm.

The augmented customer no longer compares. He delegates. Not out of laziness, but out of cognitive overload. Too many options, too many reviews, too many steps. So he lets the AI choose—just as he lets a GPS choose the route or Spotify choose the next song.

When choice is delegated, marketing becomes secondary. The only thing that matters is control over the interface that makes the decision in his place.

1.3 – UX Will Save No One

For the past decade, UX—user experience—has been the mantra of ecommerce. An almost sacred art. UX designers, UX researchers, user testing, heuristic audits, endless optimizations. UX became the promised cure for all ailments. The magic key against cart abandonment. The final defense of digital marketing.

It's a false diagnosis. UX will save no one.

Why? Because it belongs to a paradigm that is already dead—the one in which humans act on interfaces, reflect on their journeys, and decide to click. That world made sense when visitors explored, searched, and validated consciously. UX was the architect of comfort, the designer of cognitive fluidity. We optimized friction. We "put the user at the center."

But that center has shifted. The user is no longer an actor. He is traversed by a flow of predicted actions. And it is no longer the interface that rules—it is predictive intent.

You can have the most elegant UX in the world—smooth, fast, delightful—but if your user no longer needs an interface to buy, UX becomes irrelevant. It was designed for a visible world. The AI-commerce that is emerging is invisible.

Look around: voice assistant purchases, AI-driven subscriptions, pre-validated suggestions, contactless and confirmation-free payments. The customer no longer navigates. He barely authorizes. He yields. He delegates. UX becomes a polished surface on a process that no longer asks for permission.

Worse still, this obsession with UX is making us miss the real revolution. We keep thinking in terms of journeys when we should think in terms of prediction. We obsess over ergonomics when we should focus on automated decision-making. We think about interface when we should be designing infrastructure. It's a problem of perspective.

And there's a harsher truth: UX often acts as a cosmetic alibi. A distraction for brands that no longer know how to differentiate. We redesign product pages, polish micro-interactions, and run A/B tests while the fundamentals decay. The product is not distinctive. The pricing is inconsistent. The funnel no longer makes sense because the intention itself has become artificial.

UX is now the bandage on an algorithmic wooden leg—it delays the agony but prevents no collapse.

In a world where most decisions are guided by machines, UX should no longer aim to please the user. It must persuade the algorithm. The real user is no longer human. It is the predictive engine.

The UX of the future will not make buying pleasant. It will make an AI want to recommend you.

1.4 – Digital Marketing Has Become Debt

There was a time when digital marketing was a promise of freedom. Small budgets, big results. With a few dozen euros, sharp targeting, and a spark of creativity, you could generate sales. They called it "growth hacking"—it sounded clever, agile, revolutionary.

That era is gone. And no one wants to admit it.

Digital marketing is no longer a lever. It is a debt. Every euro spent today creates dependency tomorrow. Every successful campaign makes the next one more expensive. Every channel saturated by repetition becomes toxic. It is an algorithmic addiction loop: the more you spend, the more you must spend, while your control diminishes with each cycle.

Take Meta Ads. At first, they were miraculous—instant ROI, surgical precision, exponential scaling. Then, little by little, acquisition costs climbed. Organic reach collapsed. Audiences became resistant, bored, volatile. And Meta did what monopolies always do: it closed the cage.

Today, you pay for what you once had for free. You spend to maintain what was once organic. You fight to keep profitability already eroded by falling click-through rates, declining conversions, and a general public fatigue that no creative refresh can cure. It's a spiral of profitable decay.

The debt goes further. It's cognitive. Every brand that relies entirely on paid media loses its long-term instinct. It forgets how to build meaning. It replaces strategy with dashboards. Relationships with transactions. Marketers become operators of tools instead of architects of ideas.

And the debt is structural. While traditional players burn budgets on retargeting, A/B testing, and endless funnel tweaks, AI-native players do nothing of the sort. They let the machine decide—and it performs better.

AI doesn't need a 25% open rate. It measures intent at the millisecond. It doesn't send mass emails. It crafts unique messages. It doesn't test button colors. It recalibrates continuously—in real time, without fatigue, without error, without cost overruns.

So why keep fueling a system that grows weaker with every iteration, when the next level of performance lies outside your visible horizon?

The truth is, digital marketing has become a system on credit. And the bill is due.

It's no longer about pivoting. It's about changing dimensions.

As long as we think "campaign," we're already behind.
 As long as we think "segment," we're already surpassed.
 As long as we think "targeting," AI is already detecting.

And by the time we realize it, it will be too late. AI doesn't copy our methods—it erases their necessity.

1.5 – Conclusion: A Model That Fades While It Still Shines

Modern ecommerce is like a dead star—it still shines, but the light comes from the past. We continue to admire it, replicate it, believe in it, while its core has already gone cold. The model is dead, but belief keeps it alive. We are living in its afterglow.

That belief is the dream of digital commerce: accessible, agile, controllable. A world where the customer is king, data is queen, and the entrepreneur is free. But that world no longer exists. It has been consumed by rising costs, identical offers, attention fatigue, and—quietly—by the arrival of artificial intelligence.

We cling to totems: the Shopify store, the Ads strategy, the UX audit, the conversion funnel. But these totems no longer guide—they comfort. They make us believe we still control the system, when control has already shifted elsewhere.

Power now lies in recommendation engines, in language models, in generative AIs capable of producing thousands of variations in seconds. It lies in predictive systems that know your customer better than your customer service team ever could. It lies in a new grammar of commerce, where an offer no longer responds to demand but precedes it.

Traditional ecommerce still thinks it acts, but it only reacts. It plays by rules that no longer apply. It reads static dashboards while AI adjusts behavior in real time. It manages CRM while AI orchestrates emotion. It thinks "cart," while AI thinks "next intention."

This chapter is not a lament. It is a clear alarm.

If ecommerce is to survive, it must reinvent itself from the ground up. Patches won't save it. It needs a total metamorphosis—strategic, cognitive, cultural.

The old model cannot be rescued. But the next one can be built: a model that gives up control to anticipate desire, that abandons visibility to live within invisibility, that understands the future of commerce will no longer be e-, but AI-.

It is time to stop believing.
And to start seeing.

Chapter 2 – AI Is Not a Tool, It Is an Infrastructure

Introduction

One of the most damaging misunderstandings about artificial intelligence is to treat it as a mere tool—another brick to slot into place, a plugin to toggle on, an extension indistinguishable from the rest of the company's digital toolbox. It is comforting to believe that. It is also completely wrong.

AI is not a tool. It is an infrastructure.

It is not a functional overlay. It is an invisible base layer that restructures everything it touches: decision models, information systems, value flows, the relationship to customers, to the offer, and to time itself. It does not behave like an assistive add-on. It behaves like a rebuild.

You do not "do AI" by adding a chatbot, any more than you "do electricity" by changing a lightbulb. Electricity transformed industry not because it improved lighting, but because it changed the very way we produced, distributed, and planned. AI operates at the same scale.

This chapter proposes a change of lens. The question is no longer what AI can do for us, but how it redefines what we do—as entrepreneurs, merchants, decision-makers, strategists. As long as AI is perceived as a tool, it is underused, poorly integrated, and, above all, dangerously trivialized.

Understanding AI as infrastructure means accepting that it reconfigures not only our technical systems but also our mental models.

It means recognizing that it does not augment the business—it recomposes it.

2.1 – From Tool to System: Why AI Changes Scale

Across the history of technology, every major invention begins life as a tool. It is conceived to serve a specific function. The hammer strikes. The computer computes. The telephone transmits. We assign it a place, a mission, a frame. The organization integrates it where it believes it belongs. Some technologies, however, do not remain tools; they become systems. That is what artificial intelligence is doing now.

At first, AI was approached as an automation lever: to answer customers, to classify images, to predict a score. Useful functions, locally deployed. It operated within a defined perimeter, often as a complement to a human or an existing process. Then the perimeter expanded—organically, quietly, and, eventually, abruptly.

Because AI is not added; it asserts itself. It does not complete a system; it recomposes it. It is not a super-employee. It is a logic, a structure, a way of doing, thinking, and deciding. That logic is diffusing into every interstice of the company—from marketing to logistics, from strategy to execution, from back office to customer relationship.

Consider a concrete example: a recommendation engine. On the surface, it is a feature. Yet once it influences the home page, reshapes assortments, adapts prices, and steers purchases, it becomes a matrix. It transforms the offer itself. The site no longer decides what it shows; the system does. And that system can no longer be piloted by human hands alone.

Take conversational AIs as well. First perceived as support tools, they quickly become strategic points of entry. They capture attention, route flows, and interpret intention. They no longer merely answer customers. They shape them.

This is the threshold: once AI begins to influence foundational decisions—what to sell, to whom, when, and how—it exits the status of tool. It becomes a cognitive infrastructure. It decides in our place, not only to save time, but because it does the job better—faster, more finely, more efficiently. At that point, it is not an option. It is a given.

AI is changing scale because the world has changed scale. Too much data, too many variables, too many interactions. The human mind no longer suffices. Traditional management no longer suffices. Artificial intelligence is not here to accelerate an old model; it is here to instantiate a new one. It is the new model.

As long as leaders treat AI as a bullet point in a digitalization plan, they will lose. It is not a line item. It is the substrate of the plan itself.

You do not plug AI into the company. You rebuild the company around it.

2.2 – Business Models Are Not AI-Compatible by Default

The problem is not technological. It is structural.

Artificial intelligence is formidable. It analyzes, predicts, automates, and adapts. Those capabilities, however, do not create value if the underlying economic model is not prepared to absorb them. That is the chasm: the majority of current business models are not designed to function with AI.

They were engineered for a world that is predictable, sequential, and human-piloted. They rely on logics of volume, margin, budget cycles, and centralized decisions. AI introduces the inverse: instability, velocity, and decentralized micro-decisions. It fractures the cycle. It compresses hierarchies. It renders entire layers of governance obsolete.

Consider pricing. In a traditional business, price is set according to margin, positioning, and competitive study. It is adjusted periodically, often manually. A well-trained AI can continuously tailor the price of a product to the visitor's profile, the moment, the weather, behavioral history, remaining stock, and competitive pressure. This is no longer pricing; it is millisecond-level adaptive price formation. No rigid business model can absorb that without buckling.

Or take logistics. AI can anticipate flows, pre-position inventory, and trigger supplier orders predictively. If your model still runs on monthly purchasing cycles, rigid reorder thresholds, and manual picking, you will not capture the upside. You will generate data you cannot operationalize. Worse, you will produce dysfunction.

The same holds for marketing. AI can determine in real time which message, on which channel, at which moment, and with which phrasing will be most effective. If your model relies on quarterly segmentation, committee-approved campaigns, and a content plan frozen three months in advance, you are self-handicapping. You are parking a Formula 1 in a potato field.

AI demands radical flexibility from the model. Not just better tools, not just more data, but a structural capacity to operate at the speed of prediction. Very few enterprises can meet that requirement today. They tinker, they patch, they add an AI without refactoring the architecture.

That is a strategic error. AI does not improve an existing model; it short-circuits it. It resets break-even thresholds, rewrites growth levers, and reshapes cost structures. It imposes a new topology of value.

As long as business models remain linear, human-dependent, and sequential, they will be structurally incompatible with AI. AI will then be labeled "disappointing," "expensive," or "complex," not because it is any of those things, but because it is operating inside an environment that cannot receive it.

It is not AI that must adapt to the business.

It is the business that must be reconstructed around AI.

2.3 – AI Is an Invisible Infrastructure—But a Total One

Artificial intelligence does not show itself. That is precisely what makes it so powerful.

It has no façade, no easy-to-spot logo. No storefront you can point to. It is not a product you purchase or a module you toggle on. It installs itself, silently, within the deep weave of the digital economy. It infiltrates decision chains, logistics flows, pricing arbitrage, production dynamics, purchase journeys, and human relationships. It does not add itself to the business; it restructures it.

That is why AI must be understood not as a technical improvement but as infrastructure in the proper sense. It now forms the subsoil of modern operations. Like electricity or the Internet in their time, it becomes the invisible layer upon which everything rests. It redefines the conditions of action—costs, speeds, margins, trade-offs, performance gaps. It does not merely reshape practices; it alters the physics of digital commerce.

Those who hope to "adapt" their company to AI the way they adopt a new SaaS are mistaken. This is not incremental evolution. It is systemic shift. Infrastructures are not mastered through cosmetic tinkering; they force refoundation. Just as electricity did not simply accelerate steam-powered factories but required a complete reorganization of production lines, artificial intelligence requires us to reconfigure structures, roles, and decisions.

Unlike prior technologies, AI needs neither new wiring nor a physical network. It deploys within data. It operates by abstraction, inference, and correlation. It works in the margins. It filters, ranks, prioritizes, recommends, and sequences. It sculpts reality through weak signals. It turns strategy from a set of routines into an adaptive logic. It brings decisions to emergence where organizations once relied on reflex or tradition. Operating at millisecond scale, it demands reaction speeds that humans alone can no longer achieve.

As infrastructure, AI does not wait for you to adopt it. It spreads by capillarity. It is already present across your analytics, your recommendation engines, your voice assistants, your logistics platforms, your dynamic pricing modules. This is no longer a matter of anticipation; it is a present condition. And yet its ubiquity remains underestimated. Because it is invisible, it slips past attention. That invisibility is precisely what makes it inescapable.

The most common mistake is to file AI alongside CRM and CMS as just another technology. That view is anachronistic. Artificial intelligence is not an external module; it is the skeleton of the world to come. It changes the rules of the game not by adding features, but by changing the nature of the system. It erases latency, automates repetition, accelerates strategic arbitration. It follows a Darwinian logic: whatever is not optimized is absorbed; whatever can be automated is; whatever resists is forced to adapt; whatever slows the system is eliminated.

In this regime, business no longer rests on planning but on the capacity to read reality in real time. Decisions are no longer anchored in experience but in instantaneous detection of weak signals. Agility becomes the norm—not as a managerial posture, but as a continuous algorithmic response. Those who do not grasp that AI is not a tool but an infrastructure—one that imposes its laws on the entire system—will watch their model collapse without understanding why.

2.4 – Conclusion: Rebuild on AI, Not Around It

Most companies no longer reject artificial intelligence. Their real error lies elsewhere—in how they attempt to integrate it. Too often they treat it as a marginal improvement, a layer to add on top of an existing structure without questioning that structure's foundations. They treat it as an optimization tool where it demands a radical transformation. That posture reveals a deep misunderstanding of its nature. AI is not a functional supplement; it is a paradigm shift, a silent tectonics that fractures traditional landmarks.

In practice, many AI initiatives amount to bolting a conversational module onto a site, automating a few emails, or connecting a predictive add-on to a frozen CRM. These gestures do not constitute transformation. They are cosmetic bricolage—a bid for coexistence between two incompatible worlds. That coexistence will fail. AI does not graft. It absorbs. It does not complete an old model. It imposes a new architectural logic. It does not reinforce old reflexes. It renders them obsolete.

As long as AI remains confined to a technical perimeter, attached to an isolated innovation team, it remains ornamental. It is treated as a project to be managed rather than an infrastructure from which to rethink the whole. That mistake condemns countless internal initiatives to inefficiency. In today's economy, what matters are not AI projects but AI-native companies. They are already here.

These actors do not have to persuade risk-averse managers, refactor obsolete processes, or fight calcified internal cultures. They carry no technology debt and little organizational inertia. They are not trying to integrate AI into a model; their model is built on AI. Every brick of their activity rests on the ability to predict, to personalize, to iterate in real time, to remove friction before it appears. Their advantage is structural. Their scalability is native. Their agility is algorithmic.

They do not segment audiences; they capture individual intentions in every moment. They do not build strategy around AI; they carve it directly into the company's DNA. That difference changes everything. It is measured not in features but in reaction speed, adoption rate, and decision cycle. This is not a gradual transition. It is an irreversible break.

What is emerging is not just another technological wave. It is a complete inversion of priorities. Artificial intelligence is no longer a competitive advantage; it is a condition of survival. It must no longer be framed as a tool in service of strategy, but as the foundation upon which all future strategy will rest. The commerce that survives will not be the one that uses AI to optimize a sales funnel. It will be the one that eliminates the funnel, anticipates demand, treats data as the decision matrix, and redefines the act of selling as an invisible, predictive process.

It is no longer enough to think in terms of integration. We must think in terms of refoundation. Artificial intelligence does not help E-commerce. It does not support it. It is not the future extension of that model. It is its replacement. And the substitution will not happen at the margins. It will happen at the root.

Chapter 3 – Automation Does Not Kill the Human: It Kills the Mediocre

Introduction

This chapter advances a disquieting truth:
It is not progress that is violent, but the clarity it forces upon us.

For years, automation has been framed as an existential threat to humanity. With every new advance in artificial intelligence, an old fear resurfaces—the fear of erasure, the loss of meaning, a world in which machines would no longer execute but instead decide, create, and replace. That discourse, popular and imprecise in equal measure, rests on a major confusion. Automation does not endanger the human. It endangers whatever, in human work, had already ceased to be human. It does not target the person; it targets the empty function. Not the act of thinking, but the act of repeating. Not value, but mere presence.

Automation, far from being an immediate danger, is a truth test. It exposes—without mercy—what can be removed without consequence. It does not extinguish the light; it turns it back on where it had long been dark. Wherever organizations installed layers of procedure, intermediary roles, and tasks without impact, automation cuts. It flushes out the simulacrum. It trims the fat. And what it reveals is often unsettling: many people inhabit roles no longer anchored in real contribution, but inherited from a slow, fragmented, hierarchical world.

This chapter does not soften that reality. It confronts it. AI does not erase the human; it obliges us to reinvent the human. It does not destroy employment; it eliminates complacency. And within that new demand, a blunt truth emerges: only those who bring what the machine can neither compute, nor reproduce, nor convincingly simulate have a durable place in the future. Not the loudest, not the most visible. The most singular.

3.1 – AI Does Not Destroy the Human; It Reveals the Useless

One of the most persistent myths about artificial intelligence is that it erases human beings, replaces them, even obliterates them. That fear—fed by media rhetoric and dystopian fantasies—rests on a diagnostic error. AI does not kill the human. It exposes what, inside human systems, had already lost substance. It acts as a revelator, a catalyst, a mirror without indulgence. It does not create the void; it makes the void visible.

In countless organizations, whole domains of activity have survived on inertia, sheltered behind slow processes, opaque routines, and absurd norms. We have grown used to paying for functions whose sole purpose was to keep an inefficient machine turning. We normalized bureaucracy, institutionalized redundancy, and sanctified slowness. AI, by its mere presence, breaks the spell. It shows that some roles were empty shells, that some tasks existed only to keep hands busy, that certain hierarchical layers added nothing—no intelligence, no value, no intention.

Take a concrete example: handling customer requests. For years this function was carved into levels, teams, and scripts. A customer asked a question. A ticket was opened. A supervisor reviewed it. An answer was validated. A template email was sent. This theater of complexity sustained the illusion of a serious organization. Today, a conversational AI resolves most of these interactions instantly, with greater accuracy, without delay, and without fatigue. The human is not the problem. The legitimacy of the process enveloping the human is.

AI does not need a face or a personality to challenge the status quo. It has neither, and yet it sees. It sees better. It analyzes without rest. It detects weak points, redundancies, and bottlenecks. It does so without judgment. The target becomes the organization, not the individual. What the machine replaces are not people; they are roles hollowed out of substance.

This revelation is brutal not because it destroys, but because it imposes a new standard—the standard of relevance, of real value, of visible contribution. Confronted with that standard, many structures collapse because they were built on obsolete pillars. AI does not attack them; it overtakes them. It routes around them. It renders them unnecessary.

3.2 – Those Who Disappear Are Not the Ones You Think

When we discuss jobs threatened by automation, the collective imagination turns instinctively to execution roles—cashiers, drivers, switchboard operators. Visible functions, repetitive, low-skilled. That view is outdated. These are not the first to vanish. The first to go are the ones believed to be protected—the roles settled into an intellectual comfort zone, halfway between surface complexity and functional uselessness. The middling jobs. The lukewarm posts. The coordination roles without creation.

The paradox is simple: the more a function rests on relaying information, validating procedures, or producing syntheses, the more vulnerable it is. AI does not primarily eliminate manual work; it attacks the soft underbelly of organizations. That underbelly is crowded with middle managers, coordinators, analysts, report writers, and PowerPoint professionals. It is not physical work that disappears; it is simulated work.

This is not, fundamentally, a question of competence. It is a question of necessity. The market research associate, long valued for producing analyses, watches the core of that role reduced to functions that AI now performs better, faster, and at lower cost. The project manager—central in complex systems—discovers that AI manages schedules, flags risks, allocates tasks, and generates minutes. Roles once essential become optional.

The striking feature is that this disappearance does not arrive with a crash. It happens quietly. Through progressive effacement. Through gentle substitution. AI does not replace by conflict; it replaces by obviousness. It renders the role superfluous and invites a more unsettling question: what remains when the machine has optimized everything? Often, the answer is: nothing.

There is only one viable path through this transition: singularity. What cannot be imitated. What cannot be simulated. What cannot be reduced to an equation. The roles that endure are not necessarily the highest paid, the most credentialed, or the most visible. They are the ones that embody non-automatable value— nuance, imagination, human complexity. Not the generic experts. The singulars.

3.3 – Automation Restores Dignity to Work

There is a form of harshness in automation, but there is also a form of elegance. By scrubbing work of its emptiest tasks, it reveals the noble structure underneath. It reminds us that work, at its origin, is a contribution—not a position, not a title, not a bundle of mechanical duties. AI does not humiliate human work. It purifies it. It redefines it.

For decades, the world of work was parasitized by simulations of activity—pointless tasks, meetings without outcome, reports written to be forgotten, validations devoid of value. We confused complexity with seriousness. We multiplied intermediaries, tools, and decision layers. The result was a theater of efficiency running on empty. Automation cuts through the stagecraft. It reduces friction. It restores intention.

Consider a trivial but telling example: calendar management. What once required a team, assistants, reminders, and email chains is now handled in a second by an AI. The question shifts from "who will do it?" to "what sense does it make to do it manually at all?" That question replicates everywhere. If a machine can do it, why keep a human doing it? This is not an attack on the human; it is an invitation to reposition.

Where AI takes on repetition, humans can reclaim initiative. Where the machine automates the norm, humans can cultivate the exception. This shift is demanding. It requires us to exist differently—no longer through conformity, but through added value; no longer through occupation, but through tangible impact.

Automation is not a threat; it is a maturity test. It removes the mask of role and forces an answer to a simple question: what do you bring that the machine cannot bring? Asked properly, that question returns dignity to work—a dignity grounded in uniqueness, not in job titles.

3.4 – Conclusion: AI Is the Greatest Test of Sincerity in Work

For decades, the world of work told itself a comforting story: that everyone had a place, that competence, loyalty, and organization were enough, that merit was a matter of role, title, and diploma, and that whatever functioned should continue unchanged.

AI does not believe that story. It is not interested in narratives. It is interested in outcomes.

There is a harshness in automation, and there is an immense promise. Harshness, because it dissolves illusions—social protections disguised as missions, routines that only pretend to be productive. Promise, because it frees human intelligence from what suffocated it—repetition, formalism, mechanics. AI does not judge intentions; it measures results. It does not protect status; it rewards singularity. It does not grant credit for seniority; it evaluates utility. It has no loyalty, no affection, no memory in the human sense; it operates with a cold but fair logic—the logic of real marginal value.

That logic changes everything. It redefines our relationship to work, merit, and competence. It imposes a new demand: to exist inside an organization not by function, but by the capacity to produce what the machine cannot. Emotion, imagination, the texture of reality, intuition, relationship, contradiction—these are the new human territories. Everything else, in time, will be absorbed, automated, and integrated.

The shock is as cultural as it is technical. It is not enough to learn how to use AI; we must learn how to situate ourselves in relation to it—to stop hiding behind a role or a title, to stop surviving within an inefficient ecosystem. AI is not here to punish; it is here to awaken. Those who respond to this new order—not by resisting, but by reinventing themselves—will reap the gains of an era in which the human is more necessary than ever, on the condition that we be fully human.

This is not a gentle transition. It is a systemic rupture. It will not be confined to technical trades or a handful of industries; it will sweep across the entire economic fabric, every function, every organization. AI does not settle into a department; it becomes the decision infrastructure. In that environment, the only true competence is to be irreplaceable.

We must therefore abandon discourses of fear and defense. It is not automation that is unjust; it is the past systems that were. Technological progress has never killed the human. It has killed inaction, uselessness, and illusion. What automation tests is not our humanity; it is our sincerity.

We are entering an era in which work will have no value by default. It must be earned. Each day, we will need to prove that we produce something justifying the presence of a human rather than a machine. It is a historic reversal. It is a new standard. And it is a vast opportunity to rewrite what it means to work.

Chapter 4 – Those Who Control AI Control Commerce

Introduction

Commerce, in its deepest nature, has never been a neutral playing field. From its origins, it has been built upon implicit power relations, deliberate asymmetries of information, and tacit access barriers that systematically favored the best informed, the best positioned, and the most agile. These mechanisms of advantage have never been equitable. With the massive and systemic arrival of artificial intelligence, these imbalances are not merely amplifying; they are becoming structural, irreversible, and embedded in the very architecture of the market.

It is no longer enough to have good ideas, to be creative, or to execute a strategy competently. The winner is not the one who thinks the hardest, but the one who sees the fastest and the farthest. In an environment saturated, complex, and volatile, true competitive advantage no longer resides in mastering traditional levers; it lies in the ability to read the world in real time, to anticipate weak signals, and to decide before others even perceive that a decision must be made. Today, that system of reading is artificial intelligence.

AI is not an optimization utility or a technological commodity. It has become the new strategic infrastructure—the invisible yet omnipresent layer that structures perception, steers decisions, and governs flows—flows of attention, logistics, desire, cognition, and money. Whoever holds this infrastructure does not merely enjoy a technological head start; they seize the fundamental levers of commercial power.

This chapter is an alarm. Beyond its functional promises, AI is profoundly rewriting the rules of commerce. It redraws value chains, introduces massive information lock-ins, and generates unprecedented forms of algorithmic dependency. Those who master it become the new sovereigns of the digital economy; those who use it naively, or delegate its control to others, become operators under influence, reduced to reacting to decisions they no longer make.

We will explore how AI captures attention and weaponizes it commercially, why data has become the raw material of power, how algorithmic colonialism takes hold, and why refusing to build an AI strategy is akin to abandoning sovereignty over one's own business model. In this new world, failing to understand AI is not simply being late. It is becoming invisible.

4.1 – AI Captures Attention, Therefore Power

Everything begins with attention.

In a world flooded with offers, content, and messages, attention has become the fundamental currency. It is not the best product that wins; it is the one that is seen. It is not the most relevant offer that prevails; it is the one that can seize a few seconds of focused awareness in an ocean of distraction.

Attention is the most coveted, valuable, and monetized resource of the twenty-first century—not because it is rare, but because it is finite. In this cognitive economy, capturing attention precedes the creation of value.

And today, the most effective machine for capturing attention is artificial intelligence.

AI is now the most precise, scalable, and efficient mechanism for attracting and holding attention. It surpasses classic logics of targeting and segmentation. It does not wait for the user to express intent; it predicts it. It does not respond to a need; it preactivates one. By analyzing each millisecond of navigation, each mouse movement, each pause on a word, each interaction sequence, AI constructs a behavioral model that is unique, dynamic, contextual— and, crucially, operationalizable.

Under this logic, the most powerful platforms are no longer merely functional interfaces; they are attention architectures. TikTok, for instance, is not a social network. It is an AI that orchestrates micro-moments of dopamine to keep the user inside an addictive loop. Amazon is not an e-commerce company. It is a logistics AI that predicts what you will buy even before you know you want it. Google is no longer a search engine. It is an engine of intention.

Digital commerce follows the same pattern. The actor who commands AI no longer sells in the traditional sense. He configures the conditions of purchase. He does not merely present a product; he sculpts the cognitive path that leads to the act of buying. Every offer becomes a probabilistic stage set.

This process creates cumulative advantage. The more interactions an AI captures, the more finely it predicts; the more accurate its predictions, the more attention it captures; the more attention it captures, the more data it harvests. This self-reinforcing cycle erects a barrier to entry that is almost impossible to cross.

New entrants cannot simply "install an AI." They must build a data architecture, design feedback loops, and operate real-time measurement and control systems. Without these, they can only react—always a step behind, and in an economy of the instant, being behind is not a disadvantage; it is a sentence.

AI does not merely capture attention; it turns attention into power—the power to guide decisions, shape desire, and format expectations. In this new economy, not owning AI is tantamount to handing the governance of your market to someone else.

4.2 – Data Is the Raw Material of Power

Historically, economic power was built on tangible resources—land, minerals, energy, capital. Those resources were scarce, localized, extractable, and accumulable. They defined geopolitical balances of power. Today, a new form of power has emerged, founded on an immaterial, ubiquitous, yet equally strategic resource: data.

Data is not a simple residue of digital behavior. It is an imprint of intention, an indicator of interest, a conversion probability encapsulated. It reveals what mobilizes, what blocks, what motivates, what unsettles. Above all, it enables action before events occur. It makes behavioral preemption possible.

Artificial intelligence is the only infrastructure capable of exploiting this resource to its full potential. Without AI, data remains inert—a stock of numbers. With AI, it becomes a decision engine. Every signal becomes a variable, every variable a hypothesis, every hypothesis an action.

This is not technological fantasy. It is operational reality. A well-trained AI does not stop at dashboard analysis; it reads the scroll rhythm on a product page, the micro-hesitation before a click, exposure time to a banner, price sensitivity by hour of day, the emotional tenor of a support message. It transforms these micro-signals into instantaneous strategic adjustments.

AI-assisted commerce becomes a living system—self-adaptive and proactive. It no longer reacts to trends; it precedes them. It no longer answers expectations; it shapes them. The enterprise that structures its data, orchestrates it, and loops it through continuous learning gains a structural, exponential advantage that is extraordinarily hard to catch.

Power in data is asymmetric. The more you possess, the better your AI becomes; the better it becomes, the more data it lets you generate. This virtuous circle creates domination through accumulation. In such a system, the player who starts without AI does not begin with fewer tools; he begins in another era, playing a game whose rules have been rewritten without notice.

The risk is not merely commercial; it is strategic. Whoever does not own, structure, and safeguard their data—whoever hands it to others—abdicates sovereignty. They lose mastery over the customer relationship, the value promise, and the competitive edge. They become dependent on someone else's interpretive grid. That dependency carries a cost—often recognized too late to reverse.

In short, in this regime, the small player without AI is not just under-equipped; he is out of time. He participates in yesterday's game while tomorrow's rules are already in force.

And the stakes go beyond performance. He who holds the data holds the present—but more importantly, holds the future.

Because he is the one who writes tomorrow's scenarios.

Others will merely adapt to them—too late.

4.3 – The Risk of Algorithmic Colonialism

There is a more insidious danger, often underestimated by executives: cultural alignment imposed by AIs conceived elsewhere. An AI is never neutral. It carries the biases, values, and objectives of its designers. It encodes a worldview, a hierarchy of criteria, a logic of effectiveness. When that AI becomes the infrastructure of your activity, you adopt its logic—often without noticing.

Today, the vast majority of AI tools used in Western commerce are American or Chinese in origin. They were designed for specific markets, cultures, use patterns, and philosophies of performance. When a French SME relies on Amazon to sell, on Facebook to be seen, and on Google to be found, it is not merely renting powerful tools. It is renting a mental framework.

It adopts a commercial grammar where engagement trumps nuance, virality outruns veracity, and immediate performance crushes long-term meaning. It enters a system in which customer data is no longer a strategic asset, but a stream that nourishes external AIs which extract more value from it than the company itself. It becomes an operator in a game whose rules, board, and dice it does not own.

This is algorithmic colonialism—an invisible domination, accepted out of convenience or ignorance; a gradual dispossession of economic sovereignty; a willing submission to a foreign infrastructure that is often opaque and sometimes toxic.

The dynamic worsens over time. As AIs spread, they reinforce their initial biases. The more they are trained on dominant data, the more they homogenize behavior. AI does not diversify; it standardizes. It does not democratize; it concentrates. It does not liberate; it imposes.

The only viable response is to build alternatives. Develop your own AIs. Structure your own datasets. Design your own interpretive rules. This is not a nationalist whim; it is a strategic necessity. In tomorrow's commerce, those who do not master their interpretive grid will fail to perceive weak signals, miss breaks, and overlook opportunities. They will go blind inside a system they still believe they are piloting.

4.4 – Conclusion: Master AI or Be Ruled by the Market

The contemporary economy leaves no room for approximation. In this environment, artificial intelligence is neither optional nor a mere technological upgrade. It has become the skeleton of the systems that govern value, performance, and strategic direction. Those who persist in treating it as a fad or a secondary tool commit a fundamental error of reading. They underestimate not only the transformative power of AI, but the depth of the rupture it introduces into competitive mechanisms.

Every sector is now traversed by an invisible but decisive algorithmic logic. It shapes purchase journeys, anticipates behavior, sets budget priorities, and reallocates resources continuously. Human intelligence is not sidelined; it is challenged, forced to reposition itself on what only it can still produce—insight, invention, strategy. Everything that belongs to optimization, linear interpretation, or predictive management is progressively absorbed by automated systems that are faster, more precise, and more profitable.

Refusing to integrate AI into governance is not a neutral choice; it is an implicit way of recusing oneself from the center of decisions. It is ceding control of arbitrage to structures that are more agile, better informed, and able to react at the scale of the signal rather than the budget cycle. The lag is not immediately visible. It settles quietly—in eroding margins, in customers drifting away, in acquisition costs exploding, in decisions too slow to meet the market at the right moment.

Three types of actors are emerging. First, those who build their own layer of intelligence—tailored to their model, anchored in their data, capable of generating internal learning loops. Second, those who integrate lucidly into dominant ecosystems while keeping control of their critical data and decisive levers. And third, those who surrender to platforms without strategy, reduced to executing what others have already planned.

The divide is not merely technological. It is mental. It separates those who think of AI as infrastructure from those who reduce it to a toolkit. It distinguishes those who seek to understand the future from those who expect prefab solutions from AI. It pits the architects against the passive users of third-party services.

In this new world, the real question is no longer "Should we adopt AI?" but "Are we still capable of exercising strategic power without it?"

Those who do not appropriate this question will discover—too late—that they have been downgraded, not in status but in economic role. They will no longer pilot. They will be piloted.

Chapter 5 – Only Two Choices Remain: Mutate Or Die

Introduction

For more than a century, technological progress followed a rhythm that humanity could still control. Each revolution—industrial, mechanical, digital—arrived in identifiable waves. There were early adopters, fast followers, latecomers, and those who refused to change. But even the slowest could survive for a time. Transformation was progressive, not predatory. It left space to breathe, to observe, to plan, to prepare.

That world has vanished.

Artificial Intelligence has ruptured the timeline. It does not innovate—it mutates. It does not extend a paradigm—it replaces it. In the past, technology improved tools. Now, it rewires reality. AI is not a chapter in the story of innovation; it is the change of alphabet itself.

In every previous era, businesses could still rely on a safety margin—the time between discovery and adoption, between idea and impact. That margin is gone. The AI era has no latency. Between one model and the next, entire industries can disappear. Between one update and the next, entire professions can lose their meaning. Speed has become existential.

This is why traditional adaptation models no longer work. The five-year plan, the gradual transformation, the "test and learn" phase—these are now relics of a slower world. To operate under them is to drown while drawing the map of the shore. AI does not ask permission; it imposes pace.

What this book calls "mutation" is not a metaphor for modernization. It is a biological analogy for survival. Every company, every entrepreneur, every worker is now part of an ecosystem governed by evolutionary logic. Those who evolve at the speed of intelligence will thrive. Those who wait for the wave to pass will discover that the sea itself has changed.

The illusion of transition must be shattered. There is no "before and after AI." There is only "inside or outside of AI." One is a participant; the other a fossil.

5.1 – The Old Models Are Not in Crisis; They Are Dead

Across industries, executives still speak of "crisis." They describe a crisis of energy, of confidence, of purchasing power, of logistics, of attention. The word is everywhere. It sounds comforting. It implies that the system remains fundamentally sound, merely in need of adjustment. It preserves the illusion that the world has not truly changed.

But the world has changed. The so-called crises are not storms— they are symptoms. They do not announce turbulence; they announce extinction. What we are facing is not the malfunction of the machine, but the obsolescence of its design.

The twentieth-century business model—built on repetition, centralization, and linear growth—has reached its end of life. It no longer collapses in spectacular fashion; it erodes from within. Slowly. Invisibly. Like a body whose organs continue to function, but whose heart has stopped beating.

Most companies today still operate with management practices designed for the industrial age: linear planning, fixed pricing, static segmentation, manual reporting, delayed feedback. They use Excel to track performance in a world where AI makes thousands of micro-decisions every second. They build "dashboards" when the competition builds neural networks. They still believe in departments while AI dissolves boundaries.

The problem is not one of incompetence, but of architecture. These structures were designed for scarcity—of data, of access, of alternatives. The AI economy, by contrast, lives in abundance. Infinite signals, infinite context, infinite adaptation. An old model cannot survive in a new physics.

When a manager says, "We are going through a digital crisis," what they mean—often without realizing it—is that their worldview is dying. The map no longer matches the terrain. The firm still functions by quarterly cycles while its environment evolves in microseconds. The idea of a "market share" itself becomes absurd when the battlefield shifts every time an algorithm learns something new.

Calling this a crisis is comforting because it suggests a return to normality is possible. But there is no normal to return to. The post-AI world does not revert. It compounds. Each innovation builds irreversibly upon the last. There is no "pause button" for intelligence.

Recognizing this is not pessimism—it is clarity. To survive, one must first admit that the old world is gone. The sooner a leader stops fighting to "repair" it, the sooner they can start building what comes next. In evolution, denial is not a phase; it is a death sentence.

This is why the distinction between "modernization" and "mutation" matters. Modernization assumes continuity. Mutation assumes rupture. The first adds tools; the second rebuilds DNA.

The leaders of tomorrow will not be those who manage to stabilize the old system but those who invent a new equilibrium from scratch. They will not preserve their industries; they will redefine them.

Mutation, in this sense, is not merely a survival strategy—it is the new form of creation.

5.2 – Adapting Does Not Mean Using AI; It Means Thinking Like It

The greatest misconception about Artificial Intelligence is that it can be "added" to an organization—as if it were a module, a plug-in, or a digital accessory. You do not "integrate" AI. You either become compatible with its logic, or you remain outside its field of relevance. The difference is existential.

True adaptation is not technological—it is cognitive. It requires a shift from human-paced reasoning to algorithmic reasoning, from fixed planning to continuous recalibration. AI does not move linearly from cause to effect. It moves probabilistically, through endless loops of observation, feedback, and iteration. To think like AI is to abandon the comfort of sequential certainty for the volatility of perpetual learning.

Most companies still confuse automation with intelligence. They deploy chatbots, predictive scoring tools, or recommendation engines and declare victory. But that is not adaptation; it is ornamentation. An AI-ready company is not one that uses machine learning—it is one that decides like it.

To think like AI is to treat every decision as temporary, every rule as revisable, every success as data to be reinterpreted. It is to replace hierarchy with network, projection with detection, prediction with adaptation. In an AI-driven world, management no longer dictates strategy; it trains algorithms. Leadership becomes less about control and more about calibration.

This transformation is philosophical before it is operational. In the industrial age, the manager was a planner. In the digital age, a connector. In the AI age, the manager becomes an interpreter of probabilities. The new intelligence is not about perfection but optimization—reaching the best possible state given the current environment. The company that waits to "understand everything" before acting will be overtaken by one that learns through iteration.

An AI system improves because it accepts failure as feedback. Human organizations, by contrast, fear failure and delay correction. This asymmetry explains why so many incumbents fall behind: they still treat mistakes as exceptions, not as input. The cognitive gap between these two approaches widens daily.

To adapt, humans must stop imitating machines and start complementing them. AI does not have intuition, empathy, or context awareness. Humans do. But those strengths can only manifest if freed from mechanical labor. The purpose of AI is not to replace human intelligence—it is to liberate it from what makes it redundant.

Adapting therefore means redesigning the mental model of the organization. Decision-making must become distributed. Strategy must become dynamic. Learning must become continuous. AI is not a department—it is a metabolism. Every system, every person, every process must feed data into learning loops that refine themselves autonomously.

This mental revolution is far more difficult than technological adoption. Buying an AI tool is easy; becoming an AI system is not. It requires leaders who are humble enough to unlearn, and cultures capable of rewarding curiosity over certainty. The organizations that succeed will not be those that install the latest software, but those that reinvent the way they perceive, decide, and evolve.

The transformation is total: from linear to circular, from command to emergence, from optimization to anticipation. It is not about doing faster what you already do. It is about becoming something else entirely.

5.3 – The Mutation Is Not Technological; It Is Ontological

Artificial Intelligence does not merely change what we do—it changes what we are. It redefines the role of the human being in the chain of value creation. For centuries, progress meant extending human capacity outward: stronger machines, faster communication, larger storage, deeper reach. Now, progress extends inward—it replicates cognition itself.

The machine has entered the territory of the mind. It perceives, analyzes, and even predicts behavior. It does not tire, it does not forget, it does not rest. For the first time, humans coexist with a system capable of learning faster than they can understand what it has learned. This creates not only a technical challenge but an ontological one: if intelligence can exist outside biology, what remains uniquely human?

The answer is not productivity. The machine wins that contest effortlessly. What remains human is the ability to interpret ambiguity, to invent meaning, to connect the irrational with the real. The algorithm can simulate language, but not consciousness. It can generate art, but not intention. It can reproduce emotion, but not experience it.

The mutation required by this era is therefore existential. Every professional, every entrepreneur must face a simple but terrifying question: What part of my value cannot be automated? Those who answer honestly will adapt. Those who avoid the question will be replaced by those who did not.

This is not a tragedy—it is a cleansing. The automation of intelligence eliminates everything mechanical that once masqueraded as creativity. It removes the noise of procedure, the inertia of routine, the comfort of habit. It exposes the core of human work: imagination, empathy, synthesis, moral judgment.

To mutate is to move from execution to exploration. It means replacing the pride of control with the humility of curiosity. The goal is not to outperform AI on its own field—it is to operate in dimensions it cannot perceive. Intuition, contradiction, doubt, and narrative remain beyond algorithmic comprehension. The companies that understand this will not compete with AI—they will collaborate with it as a new form of intelligence partner.

This shift demands new ethics as well. When decisions are automated, responsibility cannot be. Humans must reclaim the moral dimension of intelligence. In a world where efficiency is infinite, meaning becomes scarce. And scarcity, as always, is where value lives.

5.4 – Conclusion: Mutation Is Not a Choice; It Is Survival

Artificial Intelligence does not wait for consensus. It expands, integrates, learns, and reorganizes reality faster than governance, education, or regulation can adapt. This asymmetry between technological evolution and human inertia defines the era we are living in. It is not an economic cycle—it is a cognitive one. Every organization, every individual, and every system that cannot evolve at the speed of learning will dissolve into irrelevance.

The comfort of gradual adaptation no longer exists. For decades, businesses managed change as a controlled process: define, plan, execute, optimize. AI destroys that sequence. It collapses the distance between decision and consequence. In the time it takes to discuss whether transformation is necessary, the environment has already transformed. There are no spectators in this new world—only participants and casualties.

Mutation, therefore, is not a project; it is a condition of survival. To mutate is to rebuild from within—to deconstruct the habits, assumptions, and mental architectures inherited from slower ages. It means accepting that strategy is now a living organism, that efficiency is temporary, and that relevance must be earned continuously. In evolutionary terms, adaptation was once sufficient. Now, it is too slow.

The organizations that will survive are those that learn to behave like intelligent systems—fluid, distributed, constantly reconfiguring themselves in response to new data. They do not plan the future; they prototype it. They do not defend their position; they redefine it daily. Mutation is not a crisis response; it is the default operating mode of an AI-native world.

This does not mean surrendering to the machine. It means aligning with the physics of intelligence itself. In the AI era, stability is an illusion, and rigidity is death. To resist mutation is to resist learning. To resist learning is to resist life.

Leaders must therefore evolve from managers of certainty to orchestrators of complexity. Their job is no longer to know but to sense—to detect weak signals, to navigate uncertainty, to foster ecosystems where human intuition and machine reasoning coexist productively. The future will not belong to those who control AI but to those who collaborate with it symbiotically.

For humanity, this is not a loss of relevance—it is a moment of redefinition. Every technological revolution has displaced human labor but expanded human purpose. The AI revolution will do the same, provided we accept its terms. The goal is not to compete with algorithms but to transcend them—to operate on levels of consciousness, ethics, and creation that they cannot access.

In practical terms, this means that "digital transformation" is no longer enough. The term itself belongs to a bygone age when technology was a layer added on top of an existing structure. AI demands reconstruction at the core. It is not a new tool—it is a new foundation. And that foundation requires letting go of everything that cannot evolve.

Those who cling to the past will not disappear dramatically—they will simply fade from relevance, their influence eroded by systems that learn faster than they can think. Their downfall will not be sudden but silent, hidden in the margins of lost attention, missed opportunities, and forgotten customers. The extinction of a business in the AI era is not a catastrophe; it is an unnoticed absence.

To mutate, then, is not an act of courage—it is an act of lucidity. It is to recognize that evolution has accelerated beyond comfort, and that the only stable strategy left is transformation itself. To mutate is to abandon the illusion of mastery for the truth of motion, to stop managing change and start becoming it.

The coming decade will not reward those who adapt—it will reward those who regenerate. It will belong to the organizations that rebuild themselves as ecosystems of intelligence: flexible, self-learning, self-correcting. They will not just survive—they will set the rhythm of the new economy.

AI is not asking humanity to disappear. It is asking it to evolve. It demands that we abandon the posture of resistance for the posture of invention. That we stop trying to save the old world and start designing the next one.

In the end, mutation is not about technology—it is about becoming. Those who dare to become something else will not simply endure the age of AI; they will define it. Those who do not will join the long archive of species, companies, and civilizations that mistook change for a threat instead of recognizing it for what it has always been: life continuing under a new form.

Chapter 6 – E-commerce Will No Longer Be a Website: It Will Become a Dynamic Interface Between Desire and Delivery

Introduction

For over twenty years, e-commerce has been defined by a comforting metaphor: the digital store. The website was its temple, its visible incarnation—a transposition of the physical boutique into the online world. Product pages mimicked aisles, shopping carts replaced baskets, and the "Buy Now" button became the symbolic cash register of a new era. Everything in this early digital landscape was built to reassure: clear navigation, product descriptions, trust badges, customer reviews. The merchant site felt familiar; it borrowed the mental grammar of the store and translated it into code. For a time, this illusion of continuity worked. It allowed both merchants and consumers to step into the digital age without losing their bearings.

But that world is gone. The very concept of the "site" as a place of transaction is collapsing under the weight of behavioral change and algorithmic acceleration. E-commerce can no longer survive as a *destination*. The user no longer "visits" a store; he moves through flows. His attention is fragmented across apps, feeds, notifications, and ambient interactions. He no longer seeks products—he expects them to appear, precisely when and where his desire awakens. In this new logic, the website is not the core of commerce anymore; it is a bottleneck. It slows, distracts, and demands effort. And in an economy where friction equals death, the act of asking a user to "come and browse" has become obsolete.

E-commerce is mutating. It is shedding its physical metaphors to become an *intelligent infrastructure*—a system that links intention to fulfillment with no visible interface. The transaction is no longer confined to a site; it emerges naturally from a context. A video becomes a purchase point. A voice command becomes an order. A product itself becomes a gateway. The entire idea of "shopping" is dissolving into ambient computation.

This chapter explores this metamorphosis in detail. It explains why the website, long considered the heart of digital business, has turned into its own limitation. It demonstrates how customer journeys are being replaced by predictive triggers; how products are evolving into intelligent interfaces; and how AI is transforming commerce from a reactive function into an anticipatory system.

We will see that the site is no longer the destination but the obstacle. That the buyer no longer travels through a funnel but moves in microbursts of intent. That brands must abandon the static notion of presence and embrace the fluid logic of prediction.

The e-commerce of tomorrow will not be seen, it will be felt. It will operate beneath the surface of everyday life—embedded in the content we consume, the devices we touch, the assistants we speak to. It will cease to be a place we go to and become an ambient layer of reality.

In this new paradigm, it is no longer e-commerce going to the customer. It is no longer the customer going to e-commerce. Commerce itself becomes the environment—an invisible, self-adjusting ecosystem that anticipates, reacts, and fulfills in real time.

E-commerce will no longer be a website.
It will be a dynamic interface between desire and delivery.
And this change is not on the horizon. It has already begun.

6.1 – The End of the E-commerce Site as We Knew It

The e-commerce site was one of the great illusions of the early digital age. It gave the appearance of innovation while preserving the deepest habits of traditional commerce. Its structure—categories, search bars, checkout pages—was not a rupture but a replica. It reassured more than it reinvented. It allowed the market to pretend it had changed, when in truth, it had only changed location. By rebuilding the store inside a browser, merchants transferred the old logic of the shelf into pixels. They modernized the form without transforming the substance.

This illusion was powerful. It gave birth to a generation of entrepreneurs who believed that the simple act of "being online" was progress in itself. For a while, that illusion held true. It offered reach, scale, automation. It democratized selling. But every illusion has a cost: when behavior evolved faster than technology, the structure that once liberated commerce began to trap it. The website became an administrative layer, a slow interface between desire and satisfaction. It was never meant to survive in an age of immediacy.

Today, the very concept of "navigating" a site belongs to another cognitive era. The customer no longer navigates; he reacts. He does not browse; he flows. His attention, shattered by infinite stimuli, cannot be channeled through pages and menus. In a world where each second is a decision, every additional click is an obstacle. Every form field is a deterrent. Every page load is a risk of abandonment. The site, once the gateway, has become the gate itself—heavy, static, demanding.

The digital leaders have already abandoned it. Amazon is no longer a site; it is a logistical organism powered by anticipatory algorithms. TikTok is not a network; it is an attention engine that converts emotion into transaction. Google Shopping is not a marketplace; it is a predictive index of intent. Even messaging platforms and connected assistants are transforming into points of sale without ever displaying a catalog. The interface disappears; the interaction remains.

In this new logic, the website is an anachronism. It assumes a user's willingness to travel, to search, to decide. But attention is no longer a voluntary act—it is an asset captured, modeled, and redirected. The modern consumer does not "arrive" anywhere; he exists in perpetual movement across digital layers. Commerce must follow that motion. It must abandon the architecture of the page for the fluidity of the signal.

The future of commerce is not navigational, it is relational. It does not live in URLs or menus, but in interactions, in contextual moments, in the microseconds between curiosity and conversion. The site is a static monument to a dynamic world. It cannot adapt to the velocity of the present.

Brands that continue to see their e-commerce site as the center of gravity of their digital strategy are already lagging behind. Traffic collapses because attention has migrated elsewhere—to social feeds, messaging threads, recommendation systems. The act of "visiting" a store is now as outdated as dialing a phone number to reach a friend. The real contact points have dissolved into the fabric of everyday life.

Commerce no longer needs a front door. It exists in the invisible architecture of algorithms that anticipate needs before they are expressed. The store, once a destination, becomes a dispersed presence. Not a place to go, but a network that comes to you.

The site, with its categories and funnels, is not the foundation of the new commerce. It is its fossil. Those who still worship it confuse nostalgia with strategy. The future of commerce will not be built on pages. It will be built on pulses—on the seamless transitions between seeing, wanting, and receiving.

The e-commerce site was never the revolution. It was the rehearsal.

6.2 – Buying as a Reflex: The Abolition of the Customer Journey

For years, the customer journey was the sacred framework of digital marketing. It divided the act of buying into neat, predictable stages—awareness, interest, consideration, conversion, retention. The consumer was imagined as a rational traveler moving through a series of gates, each step designed to persuade, reassure, and nudge. Marketing became the science of friction reduction. Design became the art of control. The entire architecture of e-commerce rested on one assumption: that purchase is the result of thought.

That assumption no longer holds. Artificial intelligence has not merely accelerated the customer journey; it has made it irrelevant. The path from need to purchase is no longer sequential. It has collapsed into a single moment—an impulse captured, processed, and executed by an algorithm before the buyer even realizes the thought that triggered it. Buying is no longer a process. It is a reflex.

AI observes continuously. It listens to every hesitation, scroll, pause, and swipe. It cross-references behaviors, times of day, moods, and financial capacity. It anticipates the window of receptivity before the consumer himself knows it exists. The algorithm doesn't wait for intent—it constructs it. And once the probability of action passes a certain threshold, the offer appears, perfectly timed, frictionless, self-evident. The "decision" has already been made. The consumer merely confirms what was inevitable.

The marketing funnel, with its linear precision, has been replaced by loops of anticipation. The sequence "see – think – decide – act" no longer exists. It has been compressed into "feel – react". The act of purchase emerges not from reasoning but from prediction. It does not follow a map; it obeys a trigger.

Consider an ordinary scene. A user pauses for a few seconds on a video about gardening. The system detects micro-changes in attention—tiny fluctuations that reveal interest. It correlates these signals with location, season, browsing history, and previous spending patterns. Within seconds, a contextual offer surfaces: a discount on pruning shears, one click away. There is no product page, no comparison chart, no basket. Just an instantaneous alignment between context and conversion. The act of buying occurs not at the end of a journey, but at the speed of recognition.

This is not manipulation; it is evolution. The brain itself functions on predictive coding—anticipating sensory input before it occurs. AI simply mirrors that logic at industrial scale. It translates attention into opportunity, emotion into transaction.

In this world, the concept of "guiding the customer" becomes absurd. There is no path to guide. There are only signals to interpret, probabilities to act upon. Marketing becomes the art of preemption, not persuasion. Commerce becomes a behavioral science of timing, not storytelling.

The implications are immense. Budgets shift from campaigns to models. Creative teams are replaced—or rather, redefined—as data architects. The marketer no longer crafts messages; he trains algorithms. The customer no longer experiences a brand; he interacts with its predictive shadow.

Traditional tools—CRM systems, email flows, segmented funnels—belong to a slower economy. They assume that intention precedes action. But in the age of algorithmic immediacy, intention follows action. Desire is not expressed; it is detected.

AI-driven commerce does not wait for the consumer to decide. It decides when the consumer is ready to agree. The journey is over. The reflex has taken its place.

6.3 – From Display to Prediction: The Era of Proactive Commerce

Commerce, for most of its history, has been reactive. It waited for signals. The customer expressed a need, and the merchant responded—with an offer, a price, a promise. Even in the digital age, the structure remained the same. Websites, search engines, and ads were all forms of reaction. The system answered demand, but it rarely anticipated it. The future was imagined as an improvement in response time, not a change in the nature of response itself.

Artificial intelligence has destroyed that logic. It does not wait for needs—it manufactures them. It reads patterns before they stabilize, detects desires before they are articulated, and predicts intentions before they become conscious. The new commerce no longer listens; it calculates. It operates not in response to demand, but in advance of it.

This shift is more than technological—it is epistemological. Commerce has moved from a logic of cause and effect to a logic of probability. The merchant of the past asked: *What does the customer want?* The algorithm asks: *What is the likelihood that he will want this now?* The moment the probability exceeds a certain threshold, the offer is made. Not as a proposal, but as a continuation of thought.

Consider the simplest example: the subscription to consumables. A customer buys coffee pods every three weeks. The system, trained on behavioral data, cross-references usage frequency, household size, and historical timing. Before the customer even notices the last pods running out, a message appears: "Your coffee is ready to reorder." No prompt, no search, no decision. The transaction has already been decided by a model that has learned the rhythm of the user's life.

Extend this logic beyond household products. The same predictive infrastructure can anticipate emotional or aspirational needs. It can sense fatigue, boredom, curiosity, loneliness. It can detect, from a pattern of scrolling or late-night activity, that the user is emotionally receptive to a new experience—a trip, a purchase, a change. It can connect that psychological window to a specific commercial trigger. The act of buying no longer expresses a desire. It *creates* it.

The display economy—based on visibility and persuasion—is giving way to the prediction economy, based on context and timing. The question is no longer *How do we show more?* but *When do we act?* The best offer is not the most attractive one, but the one that arrives exactly when resistance is lowest.

This predictive commerce relies on a continuous feedback loop. Each interaction generates data that refines the next prediction. Accuracy compounds. The system becomes self-learning, self-correcting, and increasingly invisible. The moment of purchase dissolves into daily life; it becomes an event so natural that it barely feels like a decision.

The traditional notion of a "market" loses meaning here. A market implies deliberation, competition, choice. But in proactive commerce, choice disappears into efficiency. The buyer no longer compares; he complies. The most effective product is not the one that competes—it is the one that arrives first.

Every sector is being reshaped by this anticipatory dynamic. Retailers plan logistics around predictive demand models. Platforms adjust pricing in real time according to micro-fluctuations in intent. Even customer service becomes predictive—resolving issues before the user notices them. The entire chain of value shifts from reactivity to proactivity.

In this world, advantage is measured in seconds. The decisive question for any company is simple: *How far ahead are you of your customer's desire?* If the answer is "not yet," then you are already behind.

Commerce has entered a regime of anticipation so advanced that the line between seduction and automation has vanished. To sell now is not to persuade. It is to appear—exactly at the right moment, in the right form, under the right conditions. And once an AI learns to predict that alignment better than you, you are no longer in the market. You are part of its dataset.

6.4 – The Product Becomes an Interface: Toward Transactional Ubiquity

In the industrial and retail eras, the product was a stable entity—an object with defined attributes, a price, a purpose, and a lifecycle that ended with purchase. Once sold, its commercial story was over. The seller moved on to the next transaction, the buyer used it, and the relationship dissolved until a new need arose. This model, long considered immutable, is collapsing. Artificial intelligence has redefined the nature of the product itself. It is no longer a static good; it is a node in a network. A data generator. A conversation in progress.

In the age of intelligent systems, every product becomes an interface between behavior and decision, between usage and prediction. It observes, records, communicates, and adapts. It turns consumption into information. And information, in turn, becomes commerce.

Take a connected hairdryer. It does not merely emit heat. It measures humidity, tracks frequency of use, and monitors wear. When airflow weakens, it alerts the customer. When filters clog, it proposes replacements. It correlates temperature settings with hair type and suggests personalized care products. It feeds data into the company's CRM, refining segmentation, triggering micro-campaigns, anticipating churn. The object becomes a salesman—not by speaking, but by sensing.

This phenomenon is not limited to smart devices. Even "dumb" products can now be integrated into intelligent ecosystems through packaging sensors, QR codes, and connected logistics. Every interaction—opening a box, scanning a label, replenishing a stock—feeds a predictive model. The act of buying transforms into a continuous loop of data, usage, and feedback. The product never stops selling itself because it never stops learning from its user.

The implications are vast. First, the boundary between product and service dissolves. A car is no longer a vehicle; it is a moving platform that monetizes attention, navigation, and consumption. A cosmetic is no longer a formula; it is a feedback device measuring adherence, satisfaction, and emotional response. Even fashion becomes an algorithmic dialogue: your shoes track movement, temperature, environment—turning lifestyle into signal.

Second, the act of sale ceases to be an event. It becomes a process. Each use becomes a micro-transaction. Each behavior is a potential trigger. The object transforms into a gateway, maintaining a constant relationship between brand and consumer. The product is no longer the end of the story—it is the interface through which the story evolves.

This shift marks the rise of what we might call *transactional ubiquity*. Commerce no longer occurs in defined spaces or times. It permeates daily life. The toothbrush that orders new heads, the detergent bottle that refills itself, the voice assistant that suggests a movie subscription—these are not conveniences; they are signals of an economic infrastructure that has absorbed routine into monetization.

As products become intelligent, the marketing cycle inverts. Instead of promoting before the purchase, brands now engage after it. Post-sale becomes pre-sale. Customer service becomes predictive. Logistics becomes cognitive. The brand's presence extends indefinitely through the product's capacity to communicate.

This evolution also raises profound strategic questions. When the object itself manages customer retention, what becomes of advertising? When usage data determines product development in real time, what becomes of traditional market research? When every product acts as both salesperson and analyst, what becomes of the marketer?

The answer is transformation. Marketing ceases to be a discipline of persuasion and becomes one of orchestration. The goal is not to sell a product but to design an ecosystem in which the product sustains its own demand. Success lies not in visibility but in intimacy—in embedding the brand so deeply into the user's environment that the distinction between using and buying disappears.

In this new model, commerce achieves omnipresence. It does not announce itself; it inhabits. It is not called upon; it responds before being summoned. The product no longer waits on the shelf or the screen. It acts. It senses. It decides. It sells.

And in doing so, it transforms the very meaning of consumption— from an act of choice to a state of connection.

6.5 – Conclusion: From Site to System, An Irreversible Metamorphosis

E-commerce is not ending. It is shedding its visible shell. What fades is not online trade itself but its old incarnation—the site, the storefront, the cart, the linear funnel. That architecture served a world in which the internet resembled a place and attention behaved like a visit. Artificial Intelligence has changed the physics. Commerce no longer rewards presence; it rewards immediacy. It no longer depends on where the buyer goes; it depends on when the system acts.

The future is not a destination but a cognition. Commerce migrates from pages to probabilities, from navigation to signals, from persuasion to timing. The store ceases to be a center and becomes a layer—ambient, anticipatory, almost invisible. Transactions emerge from context rather than from catalogues. A video becomes an order point. A voice becomes a purchase. A product becomes a sensor. The question is no longer "How do we bring customers to the site?" but "How do we meet desire before it speaks?"

In this configuration, every product is a terminal. Every interaction is data. Every signal is a potential transaction. The traditional chain— attract, persuade, convert, deliver—collapses into a closed loop— detect, predict, act, learn. Logistics, pricing, merchandising, and service synchronize in real time around a single objective: reduce the distance between intention and fulfillment to zero. What once required a journey now occurs in a moment.

Inevitability replaces visibility. The brand that wins is not the loudest but the most precise—the one whose predictive systems appear at the exact instant resistance is lowest. Identity no longer lives in slogans and homepages; it lives in behavior performed by algorithms at scale: how the system responds, how fast it adapts, how rarely it fails. Trust becomes statistical. Loyalty becomes a function of reliability rather than rhetoric.

This metamorphosis disintermediates the surface of commerce. Homepages, category trees, SEO rankings, and banner placements lose strategic weight as attention migrates to feeds, assistants, and product interfaces. The consumer no longer "arrives" anywhere; he is already inside the system. The winners will not perfect the storefront. They will engineer the substrate: data architectures, learning loops, sensing products, and protocols of presence that let the offer materialize without being summoned.

The consequences are organizational as much as technical. Marketing shifts from campaign management to model training. Design moves from pages to states. Sales teams orchestrate readiness rather than chase demand. Customer service turns predictive, preventing failure before the user experiences it. Even product development changes cadence, iterating continuously from live usage rather than periodic research. The company stops broadcasting and starts listening—at industrial scale.

This is not theory; it is already operating in the background: automated replenishment that fires before the stockout, contextual suggestions rendered inside entertainment streams, connected objects that reorder consumables, assistants that schedule and pay, dynamic pricing that tracks micro-fluctuations of intent. Each instance feels trivial; together they rewrite the grammar of buying. The interface dissolves. The act remains.

Persisting in site-centric investment as if the page were still the battlefield is to strengthen an obsolete fortification. The strategic frontier has moved underground, into models and signals, into latency and lead time. The essential question is no longer "How many visitors?" but "How many seconds ahead?" Advantage is temporal now, not territorial.

The direction is set. E-commerce evolves from surface to substrate, from store to system. What matters is not the beauty of the window but the accuracy of the engine. Not how many people see the offer, but how often the offer arrives when acceptance is highest. The most valuable capability will be the ability to disappear at the right moment—so that buying feels less like a decision and more like the world cooperating.

The roles invert. It is no longer the customer who enters the store. It is the store that enters the customer.

Chapter 7 – The Death of Traditional Marketing

Introduction

Marketing, as we once knew it, was built on an illusion: the illusion of a stable, predictable world—one that moved slowly enough for strategies to unfold, for messages to mature, and for brands to be built over time through consistency and repetition. For decades, this illusion provided comfort. The 4Ps were taught like sacred laws. Personas were crafted like living archetypes. Storytelling was treated as a universal key to persuasion—a linear narrative designed to touch vast, homogeneous audiences who would patiently listen. But that world is gone. Not because marketing failed, but because the environment that sustained it has disintegrated.

Artificial intelligence did not kill communication; it rewrote its logic. It shifted the terrain from continuity to immediacy, from narrative to signal, from persuasion to activation. The playing field is no longer temporal or hierarchical—it is real-time, adaptive, probabilistic. The marketer is no longer an author; he is an interpreter of flux. In this new ecosystem, the methods of traditional marketing are not simply outdated—they are counterproductive. They slow down what must move instantly. They attempt to tell stories to audiences that no longer listen, while machines, silently and relentlessly, learn to act before humans even realize a decision is needed.

This chapter is not a theoretical argument. It is a post-mortem. It dissects the disappearance of traditional marketing through the lens of data, automation, and predictive behavior. It reveals how the principles that once defined persuasion—message, segmentation, content, brand—have all been subsumed into a new form of intelligence. In this landscape, the goal is no longer to convince a target but to trigger an outcome; no longer to build an image but to model a response. The distinction between communication and computation collapses.

What emerges is not an evolution of marketing, but its replacement. Those who continue to think in terms of audiences, campaigns, and stories are not just behind—they are speaking to no one. They operate within a vacuum, while others, silent and systemic, orchestrate the flows of data that now capture all commercial value. The age of persuasion is over. The age of activation has begun.

7.1 – The End of Persuasion, the Beginning of Activation

For more than a century, marketing rested on one fundamental assumption: to sell, you must persuade. This idea shaped every method, every strategy, every campaign. You craft a message. You identify a target. You construct a narrative. Then you repeat it until it imprints itself into the consumer's mind. The goal was cognitive transformation—a shift in perception leading to a behavioral response. From television spots to print slogans to digital banners, the entire system was built on the same model: persuasion through repetition.

But persuasion collapses in an age where attention is the scarcest resource. Consumers no longer listen—they scroll, skip, mute, and block. Repetition no longer anchors meaning; it triggers indifference or resistance. The old narrative framework breaks under the weight of overstimulation. Meanwhile, artificial intelligence introduces an entirely new paradigm: the goal is not persuasion but activation.

Activation means that efficiency no longer depends on the message's power but on the precision of the trigger. The mission is not to seduce a mind but to provoke an action—immediately, contextually, and effortlessly. AI does not build an argument; it identifies a moment. It does not speak to an audience; it reads micro-behaviors. It detects a pause in scrolling, a shift in gaze, a half-second hesitation—and transforms it into a commercial opportunity.

This is not an evolution of marketing; it is a reversal. Content is no longer king—context is. Narrative coherence gives way to behavioral accuracy. The creative genius of the advertiser no longer matters as much as the algorithmic timing of the intervention. The new marketing does not shout—it whispers at the perfect moment. It does not persuade—it aligns.

This shift is brutal for traditional agencies. They still design storyboards while the market demands behavioral triggers. They still craft concepts while customers seek solutions that feel instantly relevant. AI-driven marketing does not narrate—it reacts. It does not plan—it anticipates. It does not theorize—it learns, tests, and acts.

The consequence is devastating for the old model: classical advertising becomes background noise—a cognitive nuisance in an environment where silence sells better than speech. The marketing of persuasion dies not because people stopped caring, but because intelligence stopped waiting. In the new order, timing is everything, and narrative is nothing.

7.2 – The Obsolescence of Personas and Segments

For decades, personas were the cornerstone of marketing methodology. Marketers invented fictional characters—semi-fabricated consumers—defined by demographic traits, motivations, and lifestyle assumptions. They served as mental shortcuts to simplify complexity. Each persona had a name, an age, an occupation, a set of habits. It was a convenient fiction, built to represent collective behavior.

But in the age of artificial intelligence, this simplification has collapsed. The persona is dead because it was never alive. AI replaces imagined averages with observed realities. It no longer speculates about the consumer—it measures him continuously. It doesn't categorize—it models. The consumer ceases to be an abstraction and becomes a dynamic trajectory—traceable, contextual, evolving.

A persona might describe "a busy professional in Paris," but the AI knows that this same person lost her job two weeks ago, has been searching meditation content late at night, and recently hesitated before completing an online order. The persona misses all of this. The machine does not. It perceives shifts in mood, variations in behavior, emotional volatility. It acts not on who you were last quarter but on what you are becoming now.

This shift turns marketing from a social science into a computational one. The marketer no longer works with categories but with probabilities. He no longer predicts behavior based on averages but calculates likelihoods based on live data. The AI says: "This individual, in this exact context, with this history, and these micro-signals, has an 89% chance of responding to this specific offer." It is not intuition. It is precision.

Continuing to use personas in this environment is like navigating an autonomous vehicle with a paper map. It is not just outdated—it is dangerous. It gives the illusion of understanding while producing irrelevant results. Campaigns built on typologies miss their mark not because they lack creativity, but because they operate in a world that no longer exists.

AI-driven marketing does not build profiles—it orchestrates reactions. It measures instead of guessing. It adapts instead of segmenting. It treats each individual as an ever-changing data model. The challenge is no longer to "know" the customer, but to track and interpret the continuous flow of who the customer is becoming.

7.3 – Content as Data, Not as Message

In the old world of marketing, content was a means of communication. It was crafted to express an idea, evoke an emotion, tell a story. Every brand believed in the power of narrative: to publish was to speak, to persuade, to seduce. Content was the brand's language, its way of existing in the collective mind. A blog post was an argument. A visual was a statement. A video was an event. Each element reinforced identity and recognition.

That conception is obsolete. Artificial intelligence has turned content from a communicative medium into a measurement instrument. Content no longer speaks—it listens. It no longer transmits—it collects. It no longer aims to convince—it exists to observe and interpret reactions. The article, the image, the video are no longer messages. They are behavioral interfaces. They are designed not to inform but to provoke measurable responses—scrolls, pauses, clicks, shares, hesitations.

Every gesture becomes a signal. A fraction of a second's delay before scrolling, a gaze fixation on a word, a linger on a frame—each micro-reaction becomes a variable in a system of continuous calibration. The AI reads these signals as data streams, feeding them back into the algorithmic engine that refines content in real time. What was once creative expression becomes adaptive experimentation. Every piece of content is a test. Every interaction, a datapoint. Every user sees a different version, shaped by their unique rhythm, device, context, and emotional state.

This dynamic marks the death of linear storytelling. There is no longer one message for all. There are thousands of variations, updated every second, invisible to the naked eye. A single article may exist in hundreds of micro-versions—its introduction, tone, or call to action adjusted by machine learning models that analyze live behavior. The marketer's role shifts from author to orchestrator, from storyteller to systems designer. The goal is no longer to make content that is beautiful or memorable, but to generate measurable effects.

In this system, content becomes the sensory organ of the brand. It detects rather than declares. It is not judged by what it says but by what it provokes. Its function is diagnostic: to reveal who the audience is, how they react, and how to move them. What used to be communication becomes computation.

The creative professional must now think like a behavioral scientist. Copywriting becomes the design of stimuli. Design becomes a form of data capture. Campaigns evolve into ecosystems of feedback loops. Every publication becomes a neuron in a cognitive network, firing signals that train the machine. This is not a degradation of creativity—it is its transformation. The most powerful creativity today is not in imagination but in iteration. It is not in storytelling but in orchestration.

AI-based marketing thus converts every act of communication into a behavioral experiment. It redefines success not by reach or visibility but by reaction density, response latency, and predictive relevance. The brand does not ask: "Did they like it?" It asks: "What did they do next?" And the answer, statistically captured, becomes the next iteration.

The marketer no longer controls the message; he controls the feedback system. The content is no longer a declaration—it is a dialogue written in data.

7.4 – The Disappearance of the Brand as a Reference

The brand was once a beacon. It gave meaning in a chaotic market. It stood for continuity, reliability, identity. Its logo condensed trust; its history created reassurance. Consumers returned because they recognized it, because it told them something stable in a changing world. The brand was a shortcut for confidence, a symbolic guarantee in an uncertain environment.

That symbolic function collapses in the algorithmic age. In a world governed by AI, recognition is replaced by relevance. The brand no longer guides choice—the system does. The algorithm no longer rewards fame—it rewards functionality. Users do not buy what they remember; they buy what performs best in the moment that matters. The emotional bond yields to the logic of optimization.

Amazon is the clearest example. It is not a brand in the traditional sense; it is an infrastructure of trust. The user returns not for the story, but for the system: the precision of recommendation, the efficiency of logistics, the absence of friction. Amazon's logo could disappear, and the loyalty would remain. The relationship is no longer emotional—it is procedural. The system itself is the brand.

Even the most powerful legacy brands are forced to mutate. Nike no longer sells aspiration through imagery alone; it integrates connected experiences, performance tracking, and personalized data loops. Apple's prestige no longer rests solely on design but on the frictionless coherence of its closed ecosystem. These are not brands—they are operating systems.

AI transforms the very nature of brand equity. It shifts value from perception to performance, from storytelling to usability, from symbol to system. In this new order, the algorithm decides which offer appears, when, and to whom. It does not prioritize heritage or loyalty; it prioritizes probability. The brand is dethroned by the metric.

This evolution also dissolves the concept of loyalty. The customer no longer returns out of attachment but out of algorithmic consistency. They buy again because the system anticipates their need faster than competitors can. Emotional fidelity is replaced by predictive dependency. The marketer's task is not to inspire trust but to maintain presence in the machine's logic.

As AI reconfigures the decision process, the brand becomes invisible. It no longer occupies the mind—it inhabits the interface. Its survival depends on systemic integration rather than narrative strength. The brands that fail to adapt to this economy of immediacy will not die with a scandal or a collapse; they will fade quietly into irrelevance, unseen and unmissed, replaced by faster, smarter, contextually omnipresent systems.

In the end, the brand's old promise—"Remember me"—is replaced by a new imperative: "You will not need to."

7.5 – Conclusion: Marketing Is Dead, Long Live the System

What we once called "marketing" no longer exists—not because it failed, but because the world that justified its existence has disappeared. Traditional marketing was an art of narration. It relied on a slow rhythm, on a linear relationship between a brand and its audience. You could plan, build, deploy, measure. The process was structured, human, deliberate. Campaigns had time to live, breathe, evolve.

Artificial intelligence has shattered that rhythm. It does not tell stories—it detects signals. It does not plan—it anticipates. It does not speak—it acts. Marketing is no longer a creative discipline but a behavioral science. The goal is no longer to convince—it is to trigger. The heart of the system is no longer the message—it is the moment. It is not the story—it is the effect.

This transformation is irreversible. It reflects a new anthropological reality: the modern user does not wait for a brand to speak. They expect a solution to appear. They no longer care who provides it, as long as it works, immediately, seamlessly, invisibly. Artificial intelligence, with its ability to model behavior, predict intention, and automate reaction, has become the infrastructure of modern marketing.

The marketer's role is now unrecognizable. No longer the architect of messages, but the engineer of systems. No longer the designer of campaigns, but the orchestrator of activation flows. No longer the builder of images, but the optimizer of decisions. Marketing has been absorbed by the machine. What used to be called creativity has merged with computation. What used to be called strategy has become architecture.

Those who still try to shout their slogans into the void of mass audiences are speaking to no one. Their audience has fragmented into a million micro-moments, and their message is lost in the noise. Meanwhile, those who understand that marketing is now an automated decision process—those who can synchronize technology, data, and timing—capture all the value, silently.

The future will not belong to advertisers. It will belong to analysts, coders, and architects of experience. The marketing of tomorrow will not be a department of communication. It will be part of the company's digital nervous system—integrated, invisible, and infallibly efficient.

This is not an update. It is a replacement. Marketing, as we knew it, is dead.
And what replaces it no longer needs a name.

Chapter 8 – Artificial Intelligence: The New Commercial Infrastructure

Introduction

Artificial intelligence is still too often seen as a technological lever, an efficient add-on meant to optimize existing processes—automation, content generation, personalization, scoring. This perception, as common as it is reductive, reduces AI to a functional accessory, a tool serving an unchanged system. It is attached to obsolete structures as if it did not transform their logic entirely. But this view is dangerously wrong. Artificial intelligence is not an additional layer; it is the foundation of a new paradigm. It is not a technology to be implemented but a logic to be embraced—or suffered.

To think of AI as infrastructure is to understand that it redefines economic dynamics, human roles, decision cycles, and organizational models from the ground up. Like electricity in its time, AI does not simply improve what we already do—it transforms the way we think and act. It does not offer incremental efficiency; it imposes a complete reinvention of the foundations.

This chapter demonstrates why artificial intelligence has become the backbone of modern commerce. It explains how AI transforms companies into cognitive ecosystems, distributes intelligence across every operational layer, becomes the new energy of business, and why rebuilding on this foundation is no longer optional but vital before current structures collapse under their own weight.

8.1 – An Infrastructure, Not a Feature

Most companies still view AI as a tool—a means to optimize a specific task. They adopt it as they once did CRMs, chatbots, or accounting software. This reveals a profound misunderstanding: artificial intelligence is not a component added to an existing structure; it is a structure in itself. It does not complement the architecture of yesterday—it replaces it.

A retailer who uses AI merely to write product descriptions faster has changed nothing; they have only accelerated a process. But a retailer who entrusts algorithms with dynamic pricing, stock management, personalized offers, predictive logistics, and returns processing has not just optimized commerce—they have transformed its nature. They no longer sell as before; they sell differently, because they think differently.

AI operates continuously, upstream from human decision. It does not wait to be instructed; it observes, detects, anticipates, proposes, adjusts, and executes. It is not an auxiliary intelligence; it is a proactive one. It positions itself at the core of the organization, capturing weak signals, reconfiguring responses, and adapting in real time. It follows no fixed procedures; it builds dynamic models that evolve at the speed of context.

Within this new paradigm, leadership itself changes nature. The executive no longer controls activity—they define the rules of the system. They set objectives, parameters, and thresholds. They arbitrate exceptions. The rest operates autonomously. The marketer no longer plans static campaigns but orchestrates adaptive scenarios rooted in continuous learning. The salesperson is no longer a persuader but the human interface of an algorithmic recommendation system.

This transformation is profound and irreversible. Those who fail to grasp it will soon face the same fate as booksellers before Amazon, taxi drivers before Uber, or travel agents before Booking.com. They will not be outpaced by technology but by their own immobility.

8.2 – The Company as a Cognitive Ecosystem

Traditional enterprises were built on a Taylorist worldview: linear processes, rigid hierarchies, and centralized decision chains. Each task was isolated, each department sealed, each decision validated through layers of management. That model once ensured industrial efficiency. Today, it ensures obsolescence.

Artificial intelligence replaces this mechanical vision with an organic one. The company becomes a living, sensing ecosystem. It perceives, interprets, acts, and learns. It functions like a nervous system—each interaction becomes a signal, each data flow fuels a model, each action generates feedback that refines the next response. The loop is continuous, decentralized, and self-adaptive. There is no longer a single command center; intelligence circulates through the entire network.

In such an environment, organizational silos collapse. Marketing is no longer a department—it becomes a function distributed across the entire user experience. Logistics is no longer a back-office operation—it is a constellation of feedback loops optimizing every flow in real time. Strategy is no longer determined once a year behind closed doors—it evolves daily, recalibrated by signals captured by the system.

The human role changes radically. Humans no longer execute— they interpret. They detect anomalies, identify blind spots, and ask the questions machines cannot yet formulate. They no longer stand at the center but at the intelligent periphery, where sense-making and creativity remain irreplaceable. They no longer manage the system—they nurture, question, and steer it.

A cognitive company is defined not by what it produces, but by how it learns. Its strength lies in its ability to model its environment, to adapt instantly, to extract meaning from noise, and to transform data into relevant action. It is not smarter because it stores more information, but because it converts that information into decisions faster and with greater precision than competitors.

This model is not a luxury reserved for digital giants. It is a condition of survival. In a volatile, accelerated, and opaque world, only those capable of learning faster than their environment will endure.

8.3 – Distributed Intelligence: The End of Centralization

Until recently, corporate power was synonymous with centralization. Decisions originated at the top, filtered down through layers of management, and were executed by those below. Information traveled upward slowly; validation trickled downward even more slowly. It required meetings, dashboards, and approvals. This model was stable, but it was also inert—a product of an age when predictability was the rule. That age is over.

Artificial intelligence has broken this hierarchy. It distributes operational intelligence to every node of the system. Each part of the network can now analyze, decide, and act autonomously within defined parameters. A recommendation engine does not need a marketing plan to propose the right product—it observes, tests, and adjusts in real time. A customer service chatbot no longer waits for managerial approval to respond—it learns from interactions, detects sentiment, and tailors its tone instantly. A supply chain system no longer requests validation before redirecting shipments—it recalibrates its flows automatically based on predictive models.

This is not chaos; it is systemic intelligence. Control does not disappear—it changes form. Leadership no longer dictates each move but defines the framework in which decisions are made.

Instead of micromanagement, there is architecture management. Instead of orders, there are learning protocols. Instead of monitoring execution, leaders monitor adaptation.

The benefits are radical. Friction disappears. Speed increases. Latency collapses. The organization becomes more agile and resilient: when one node falters, others compensate automatically. Redundancy becomes strength. Flexibility becomes structure. The human contribution shifts from controlling to designing the boundaries of autonomy.

But such distribution of intelligence demands a profound cultural shift. It requires leaders to let go of the illusion of total control. To accept that not everything must be understood, supervised, or validated. To trust systems—not as tools, but as intelligent collaborators. For many organizations, this is the hardest transition of all: replacing the culture of command with the culture of calibration.

Yet this is the only way forward. Centralized organizations are too slow for an environment that evolves by the second. The future belongs to distributed systems—fast, adaptive, self-correcting. Intelligence is no longer concentrated; it is diffused. And in that diffusion lies both efficiency and survival.

8.4 – AI as the New Energy of Commerce

Every great economic revolution has been driven by a dominant energy. Coal powered industry. Electricity powered automation. Digital connectivity powered globalization. Today, artificial intelligence powers cognition itself—it becomes the energy of thought, the engine of anticipation, the fuel of commerce.

Unlike previous energies, AI is not consumed—it accumulates. It does not deplete—it amplifies. It does not heat—it computes. It permeates every function of business: marketing, logistics, finance, customer relations, manufacturing. It flows invisibly through all processes, transforming them into learning systems.

A website powered by AI is not a static catalog; it is a living organism. It selects what to display according to behavioral profiles, adjusts prices based on demand elasticity, predicts needs from micro-patterns, and adapts tone and content in real time. A warehouse guided by AI does not store—it orchestrates. It optimizes locations, routes, and inventory turnover, predicts surges in demand, and prepositions goods before shortages occur. Even customer experience itself becomes energetic: every interaction becomes a data point, every hesitation a signal, every choice a recalibration.

This energy is available to all, but few know how to harness it. AI does not activate through the purchase of software—it activates through vision. It requires architecture, coherence, and culture. It demands the redesign of flows, roles, and priorities. It requires leaders capable of thinking in systems rather than hierarchies, of seeing data not as reports but as movements of energy circulating through their organization.

Those who master this flow achieve commerce that is fluid, predictive, and resilient. They no longer react—they preempt. They no longer follow trends—they generate them. Those who fail to adapt remain trapped in outdated cycles of planning and correction, perpetually one step behind.

Artificial intelligence is not an accessory to business—it is its bloodstream. It transforms companies from mechanical engines into cognitive organisms. It is not the next revolution in commerce. It is the end of the old one.

8.5 – Conclusion: Rebuild Without Nostalgia

Those who still treat artificial intelligence as a strategic option are misreading the era. It is not a choice—it is a mutation. AI is not an additional asset; it is the new foundation. It is not a technology to integrate—it is the architecture upon which everything now rests.

Commerce built on segmentation, planning, annual campaigns, and top-down decisions is already obsolete. It is slow, rigid, and inefficient. It cannot compete with adaptive systems that learn continuously, optimize autonomously, and operate at the speed of context. There is no catching up for those who cling to the past; the system itself has moved on.

This transformation demands more than modernization—it requires deconstruction. The old structures must be dismantled to make room for intelligence that circulates freely. Less hierarchy, more modularity. Less planning, more learning. Less control, more algorithmic supervision. Less storytelling, more measurable effect.

Those who delay this transition believe they are buying time. In reality, they are losing it. Their competitors are no longer the same; they are invisible, decentralized, and algorithmically driven. They have no brand, no face, no voice—but their precision, speed, and adaptability will crush any organization that still operates on legacy logic.

This is not a question of trend or technological enthusiasm. It is a question of survival. The commercial world no longer runs on promises—it runs on systems. The difference between those who thrive and those who vanish will no longer depend on creativity, charisma, or tradition. It will depend on who masters the infrastructure of intelligence.

Artificial intelligence is not the tool of commerce. It is its condition of existence. The companies that will define the next decade will not be those that use AI, but those that think, build, and breathe with it. Those that hesitate will soon realize that by the time they finally decide to adapt, the market will already have evolved into something else—something they no longer understand.

To rebuild without nostalgia is the only viable path forward. The past cannot be repaired. It must be replaced. Those who understand this will not merely survive the mutation—they will define its rules. Those who hesitate will fade, victims not of technology, but of their refusal to evolve. The age of strategy is over. The age of systems has begun.

Chapter 9 – E-Commerce Is Dead, Long Live Intelligent Commerce

Introduction

E-commerce was once hailed as the apex of digital capitalism—a promise of accessibility, immediacy, and freedom. It appeared to unite technology and consumption into a single, frictionless experience. At its birth, it disrupted the physical circuits of distribution, overturned geographic limitations, and reinvented the very notion of the store. For two decades it symbolized modernity, growth, and the digital future. It was celebrated, theorized, financed, and idealized. Yet hidden beneath this enthusiasm lies a fundamental misconception: e-commerce was never the end of the story. It was merely an evolutionary phase, and that phase has already expired.

The true revolution was not the Internet but the rise of intelligent systems capable of perceiving, anticipating, and acting before intent is consciously expressed. E-commerce digitalized existing trade; artificial intelligence redefines the essence of commerce itself. It transforms the marketplace from a visible transaction space into an invisible activation network. The click becomes an artifact. The cart, an anachronism. The act of buying turns into a fluid continuum that requires no deliberate action.

This chapter is not an obituary; it is a clinical dissection. The aim is not to proclaim the death of e-commerce, but to recognize its strategic obsolescence. Locked within linear paradigms, the model has become too slow, too visible, too rigid. It no longer reflects how needs arise, evolve, or are fulfilled. Facing it stands a new paradigm: intelligent commerce—autonomous, ubiquitous, predictive. A form of commerce that no longer waits for the customer's initiative but activates itself, often silently, within the flow of daily life.

9.1 – E-commerce as an Outdated Model

The rise of e-commerce was dazzling. It offered the illusion of infinite choice and frictionless access. It promised liberation from physical constraints, personalized experiences, and global reach. For years that illusion fueled exponential growth. But beneath its surface, the model was already eroding. E-commerce rests on a fiction: the rational, self-directed consumer who searches, compares, and decides. That consumer has vanished.

Today's users no longer want to browse; they want to receive. They no longer seek; they expect. In an economy saturated with stimuli, the promise of freedom has turned into a cognitive burden. Each additional option drains attention. Each extra click provokes fatigue. Each layer of navigation becomes an obstacle. What once signified modern convenience now feels like friction.

Conversion rates reveal the truth. Despite billions invested in UX, analytics, and optimization, most visits end without purchase. The issue is not desire but exhaustion. The system demands too much effort—too many micro-decisions in an environment of distraction. Attention has become a currency too precious to spend.

Meanwhile, the marketplace has hardened into a battleground of marginal improvements. Faster delivery, easier returns, cleaner design—all micro-wars fought for fractional advantage. None restore meaning or emotion. The structure itself is obsolete: a static interface addressing a moving target. Consumers, overwhelmed by abundance, drift toward simpler, predictive experiences where effort disappears.

E-commerce no longer astonishes; it administrates. It has become an institution—a bureaucracy of buttons, funnels, and pixels. Institutions, once stabilized, decay. To believe e-commerce still represents progress is to mistake persistence for vitality. The next transformation will not emerge from improved platforms but from systems that eliminate the need for platforms altogether.

9.2 – Intelligent Commerce: An Autonomous System of Activation

Intelligent commerce is not an improved version of e-commerce. It represents a complete anthropological rupture. The objective is no longer to make the act of purchase simpler or faster—it is to make it almost invisible, seamlessly integrated into daily life, triggered by a continuous environment of data, signals, and contextual awareness. The customer is no longer a visitor navigating a store; he becomes the living center of a network of interactions that interpret, anticipate, and act on his behalf.

In this architecture, the storefront disappears. The product is not presented—it is suggested, integrated, delivered. Intention is no longer expressed—it is inferred. The act of purchase is no longer a choice—it is a reaction. Every movement, pause, or silence becomes a measurable signal. Weather patterns, vocal tones, heart rate, geolocation, sleep quality, stress levels—all combine to form a constantly evolving behavioral profile. This profile becomes the foundation of a decision-making engine that initiates commercial actions not reactively, but preemptively.

Netflix does not ask what you want to watch—it already knows. Spotify does not inquire about your mood—it senses it through your rhythm and listening habits. Amazon does not wait for a click—it prepares the order before you even realize you need it. That is intelligent commerce: not an enhanced interface, but the disappearance of the interface itself. The need becomes the trigger; the action becomes the response.

In this context, the role of the merchant changes profoundly. It is no longer to build websites, craft email campaigns, or schedule promotions. It is to design architectures of activation—systems that connect micro-signals to instant decisions. The modern merchant is not a storyteller; he is a systems architect. He operates not with messages but with models, not with images but with variables, not with planning calendars but with probabilistic windows of opportunity.

This shift redefines the very identity of commerce. Selling is no longer about persuasion; it is about precision. Competition no longer rewards visibility but context. The decisive factor is not who shouts the loudest, but who triggers first. And in a world where milliseconds decide outcomes, the fastest algorithm replaces the most creative slogan.

Intelligent commerce is not a theoretical horizon—it is already here. It thrives within connected objects, silent apps, voice assistants, banking APIs, and satisfaction algorithms. It spreads unnoticed, replacing the effort of choice with the efficiency of automation. The future of selling is not in talking more effectively to customers, but in acting for them—before they even think to ask.

9.3 – From Interface to Infrastructure

For over two decades, digital commerce was designed around interfaces: websites, mobile apps, conversion funnels. Everything was visible, structured, and meticulously engineered to lead the user toward one final goal—the click. Entire industries emerged to perfect that journey. UX designers, CRO consultants, analytics experts—all devoted their expertise to making the interface as smooth as possible. And it worked—until behavior changed.

Today, the interface is no longer central. It is a commodity. Consumers do not want to "browse" or "explore." They simply want outcomes—instant, seamless, reliable. Value no longer resides in the visual layer but in the invisible infrastructure that enables ultra-contextualized experiences. The future of commerce does not depend on what users see, but on what happens without them noticing.

The modern enterprise must therefore pivot. It must stop building façades and start building systems. Investment must shift from pages to flows, from aesthetics to anticipation. What drives performance is not how beautiful the store looks, but how precisely it adapts to context. E-commerce was a stage; intelligent commerce is a neural network.

This network is made up of APIs, rule engines, real-time data pipelines, behavioral databases, and adaptive learning models. It operates behind the curtain—detecting, evaluating, and adjusting. Above all, it evolves autonomously. Each user receives a different version of the experience, because each user is processed as a unique signal in a living system.

Such a paradigm requires a complete rethinking of architecture. The monolithic systems of the past must give way to headless platforms, microservices, event orchestrators, and embedded decision engines. Commerce becomes a self-adjusting platform, capable of mutating in real time without human intervention.

This is not only a technical evolution—it is a cultural one. Running such a system demands letting go of total control in favor of managed uncertainty. It means trusting adaptive intelligence over static planning. It means designing for evolution, not perfection. The new mindset is humble, analytical, and quiet.

Commerce no longer needs to be seen to exist. It operates in the background—efficient, anticipatory, invisible. What once required attention now runs on intuition. The store of the future does not open its doors. It opens possibilities.

9.4 – The Disappearance of the Purchase Moment

One of the paradoxes of digital commerce is that it turned the act of purchase into a ritualized event, a peak moment of supposed satisfaction. The click, the validation, the confirmation email—each step was designed to produce a sense of accomplishment, as if buying were an achievement rather than a necessity. The e-commerce industry built its temples around this sequence, optimizing every detail through persuasion techniques, scarcity effects, and social proof. Yet in the age of intelligent commerce, that moment vanishes—not by accident, but by design.

Consumers no longer want to buy; they want to obtain. This is not a nuance of vocabulary but a shift of civilization. To buy means to decide—to search, to compare, to act. To obtain means to receive— instantly, effortlessly, and naturally. The buyer's role dissolves into the system. What remains is pure utility: an automated satisfaction of needs before they are even articulated.

Consider a simple case: a user consumes coffee capsules at a predictable rhythm. The connected machine counts usage. The algorithm detects depletion. A reorder is triggered automatically. The user does not choose, does not confirm, does not even think. He is simply supplied. This model already exists, and not just for consumables. It extends to health, mobility, insurance, and energy. Any process that can be modeled can be automated.

In this logic, traditional marketing collapses. There is no story to tell, no persuasion to deploy. The art of selling is replaced by the science of calibration. The goal is no longer to make people want, but to ensure that what they need is already there when the need arises. The merchant becomes a designer of trust systems—structures that guarantee continuity, reliability, and frictionless experience.

The "purchase experience" becomes secondary, almost obsolete. There is no longer a tunnel to optimize or a conversion funnel to perfect. The act of buying disappears into the background, replaced by continuous synchronization between desire and delivery. It becomes an environmental effect rather than a consumer initiative.

This disappearance also shatters traditional performance metrics. Conversion rates, ROI, campaign effectiveness—all lose meaning when the transaction itself is automated. What matters is not how often the client buys, but how rarely he has to think about buying. The true KPI becomes silent satisfaction: the invisible alignment between system action and human expectation.

In this new paradigm, the brands still trying to seduce will vanish behind those that have learned to disappear. The future does not belong to those who advertise best, but to those who remove the very need for advertising. The less the user notices the act of purchase, the more successful the system becomes.

9.5 – Conclusion: The Burial of E-commerce

E-commerce, as we know it, will not die in an explosion. It will fade, quietly, like an obsolete protocol still running in the background. It will survive as a residual structure—a refuge for complex transactions, a fallback for hesitant users, a nostalgic space for human decision-making. But it will cease to define the norm. Like the fax after email, or the DVD after streaming, it will persist without purpose, tolerated but irrelevant.

The true challenge now is not to perfect an outdated mechanism but to transcend it. The future of commerce will not be built on interfaces, pages, or funnels. It will be structured on invisible infrastructures powered by AI—fluid, predictive, and adaptive. The storefront will dissolve into data flows. The product page will become a behavioral model. The act of selling will merge into the logic of service.

This disappearance is not a loss. It is liberation. The end of attention warfare, of the tyranny of clicks, of algorithmic exhaustion. It is a return to the essence of commerce: to serve. In an ecosystem where purchasing becomes a silent continuity, true value lies in the precision of intervention—the ability to deliver without disturbance, to act without intrusion.

But this evolution demands a total reconstruction. Cultural first: shifting from "customer thinking" to "usage thinking." Technical next: abandoning page-based systems for event-driven architectures. Strategic finally: renouncing visible metrics in favor of real, frictionless outcomes.

The threat is not to e-commerce as a technology—it is to the very idea of visible commerce. The consumer of tomorrow will no longer buy. He will obtain. He will no longer compare. He will receive. He will no longer click. He will live within responsive systems that anticipate his every need.

The merchant's new role is not to stand before the customer but to disappear behind the experience. Success will no longer mean being seen, but being perfectly, invisibly present—exactly where and when life happens. The true frontier of commerce is not the store. It is life itself. And in that life, artificial intelligence is already selling—quietly, efficiently, invisibly—long before we notice it has arrived.

Chapter 10 – The Death of the Conversion Funnel

Introduction

Digital marketing was built on a comforting illusion: the conversion funnel. In this model, the user progresses through neat, logical stages. They enter through the wide door of awareness, move along the corridors of consideration, reach the chamber of decision, and emerge as loyal customers. For two decades, this diagram structured every marketing practice—tracking tools, content strategies, user interfaces. It industrialized the act of selling in the digital age. Yet it no longer works.

The problem is not technical obsolescence but conceptual distortion. The funnel assumes a sequential, rational progression that no longer exists. The digital consumer no longer advances along a path—they drift through an infinite set of micro-bifurcations. Flow has replaced journey. Attention is fragmented, mobile, contextual. The decision to buy no longer emerges from a linear process but from a convergence of fleeting conditions.

Artificial intelligence does not try to push users through a tunnel. It identifies, within chaos, the precise conditions that make an action probable. It captures the instant when latent intention becomes explicit behavior. This is more than a methodological revolution—it is a cognitive one. The merchant's role is inverted: no longer a designer of journeys, but an explorer of signals. They do not lead traffic—they detect emergence.

This chapter is not an ideological rejection of the funnel; it is a clinical observation of its end. The model is too slow, too rigid, too sequential. It assumes a rationality that human behavior has abandoned. And above all, it prevents AI from doing what it does best—modeling the unpredictable.

10.1 – The Myth of the Rational Journey

The conversion funnel rests on a useful fiction: that of a rational consumer progressing logically through predefined stages. The notion was seductive because it brought order to complexity. It made behavior predictable, interfaces measurable, strategies quantifiable. Marketing became mechanical—a form of engineered desire.

Reality, however, has shattered the myth. The user is not a marble rolling down a slide but a drifting particle influenced by context, mood, and impulse. They browse products between two subway stops. They close a tab to answer a message. They encounter the same brand weeks later in a random post. They click without intention and buy after watching a TikTok they barely remember. Nothing follows a straight line.

Digital behavior is not a road—it is fog. The buyer moves by instinct. The rational journey is a comforting abstraction, not an anthropological truth. Even the concept of "intention" has dissolved: no longer explicit, no longer stable, no longer directional.

This chaos is where AI thrives. It does not analyze steps—it detects patterns. It does not follow progression—it recognizes probability fields. It reads signals invisible to human marketers: scrolling speed, cursor hesitation, micro-pauses, eye fixation, erratic navigation rhythms. Each behavior, meaningless alone, becomes powerful in aggregate.

The funnel ignores these micro-events. It waits for form submissions, page views, and clicks. It is deaf to ambiguity and blind to implicit intent. It cannot process nuance. But AI can. The merchant's task is no longer to guide users down a path—it is to cast a probabilistic net, capable of capturing intention wherever it surfaces. The straight line gives way to a mesh of opportunities, where every interaction is a potential entry point.

10.2 – Probabilistic Marketing: A Silent Revolution

Abandoning the conversion funnel does not mean abandoning structure—it means evolving toward a new logic: probabilistic, distributed, adaptive. In this model, each user is not a traveler but a constellation of signals, some of which converge into action.

The goal is no longer to push someone from point A to point B, but to estimate the probability that an action will occur at time T, within a given context, under the influence of a micro-stimulus. It is not persuasion—it is precognition. This precognition operates through systems that learn in real time.

The tools reflect this shift: behavioral scoring engines, predictive models, event-driven orchestration, real-time databases. Segmentation gives way to dynamic clustering. Funnels give way to scenarios. Campaigns give way to autonomous triggers activated when probabilities reach critical thresholds.

The marketer's role transforms accordingly. They are no longer storytellers but conductors. They design not messages but mechanisms. They plan not campaigns but conditions. And they must learn to relinquish control. Probabilistic marketing is, by nature, nonlinear, volatile, and uncertain—but it works, because it mirrors the way humans actually behave.

It synchronizes rather than pressures. It listens rather than insists. It acts when timing aligns instead of forcing intent. It lowers cognitive friction, increases perceived relevance, and restores natural fluidity.

This is a silent revolution—but a total one. It reshapes tools, cultures, and hierarchies. It replaces strategic planning with adaptive orchestration, persuasion with precision, prediction with synchronization. In this world, purchase is no longer the end of a path—it is a distributed event, a statistical consequence of the right conditions.

10.3 – Action Instead of Attention

Traditional marketing was founded on one sacred principle: to sell, one must first capture attention. This belief shaped the entire advertising industry, built the giants of the digital era, and justified endless campaigns devoted to reach, exposure, and brand awareness. But in a world where every second of concentration is contested, attention has become a lost battlefield—too fleeting, too fragmented, too expensive, and, above all, unnecessary.

The objective is no longer to capture attention. It is to trigger action.

The shift is simple yet profound: modern buyers do not want to be convinced—they want things to work. They do not seek persuasion; they seek frictionless efficiency. The new marketing logic is not to stimulate reflection, but to remove resistance. The intelligent system must know its users so precisely that it acts on their behalf at the right time, without interruption, without noise.

This is why the most advanced brands no longer produce campaigns. They build activation architectures. A personal stock drop, a change in usage rhythm, a new location, a deviation from a behavioral pattern—each of these becomes a signal to act. It is no longer the user who initiates; it is the system that anticipates. A relevant notification appears, a prefilled order is proposed, a recurring purchase is executed. The transaction becomes reflex, not through persuasion, but through optimization.

Interfaces evolve accordingly. No more complex forms or multi-step validations. Experience becomes minimal: one gesture, one word, one confirmation. The interface fades. Commerce becomes ambient.

This transformation redefines the merchant's mission. The goal is no longer to attract but to integrate. The best experience is the one that does not interrupt. The right moment outweighs the right message. Implicit action replaces explicit engagement. Traditional metrics—click-through rate, bounce rate, session duration—lose meaning. The only metric that counts is the action executed, not the attention measured.

The user no longer wants to watch. They want it done.

And this shift is not marginal—it is civilizational. The successful commerce of tomorrow will not be the loudest or most visible, but the most frictionless. The winners will not capture attention. They will make it irrelevant.

10.4 – Personalization Is No Longer Enough

For years, personalization was digital marketing's holy grail. Addressing customers by name, recommending products based on past behavior, tailoring offers by segment—all once felt magical. But that magic has vanished. Personalization has become the norm—and, worse, a form of laziness.

Customers are no longer impressed by being recognized. They expect it. And when an expectation becomes universal, it ceases to create value. Static personalization now feels cosmetic: decorative, predictable, hollow. It flatters the ego but achieves nothing.

In intelligent commerce, such personalization is not just insufficient—it is counterproductive. What matters is not tailoring the message, but tailoring the behavior. Not sending a targeted offer, but triggering the right action at the right moment. The goal is no longer to speak to the user but to act for them, silently, before awareness arises.

This represents a radical paradigm shift. Marketing no longer segments; it detects. It no longer schedules campaigns; it orchestrates occurrences. It no longer programs scenarios; it lets algorithms adapt and learn. The marketing department becomes a real-time system of behavioral alignment. It no longer addresses static personas but fluid cognitive states, modeled dynamically by AI.

This requires new infrastructure—high-frequency data capture, contextual prediction engines, generative algorithms, distributed orchestration frameworks. But even more importantly, it requires a new mindset. Marketing ceases to be the art of messaging. It becomes the science of decision-making. The mission is not to seduce but to activate.

Visible personalization is dead. It is slow, predictable, superficial. AI enables invisible personalization—probabilistic, contextual, adaptive. It does not tell the customer "I know you." It demonstrates it—by acting faster, smarter, and more accurately than they could. It reduces friction. It anticipates intention. It eliminates effort.

And this new standard tolerates no approximation. It demands precision, timing, and reactivity. The brands still stuck in the decorative phase of personalization will fade into irrelevance. Those that master implicit activation will dominate.

The race is no longer about creativity. It is about responsiveness.

10.5 – From Journey to Pattern: The End of Linear Marketing

The conversion funnel once had pedagogical value. It gave marketers a framework, a sense of structure, and an illusion of control. It turned complexity into sequence, chaos into method. But that structure was only ever a simplification of reality. The truth was always messier, more erratic, more human. Today, the structure collapses completely. The straight line dissolves into a field of fluctuations. Marketing must now confront reality as it is—nonlinear, unpredictable, fluid.

In this new reality, the goal is no longer to organize a path. It is to detect patterns. These patterns—behavioral motifs, recurring micro-tensions, subtle repetitions of digital gestures—contain the essence of intent. Intention no longer lives in pages viewed or carts abandoned. It lives in frequency, hesitation, rhythm. The marketer's task is to read the invisible choreography of behavior, not to shepherd users through predetermined checkpoints.

Artificial intelligence is built precisely for this. It does not explain; it detects. It does not interpret what the user says they want; it models what they will probably do. It does not tell stories; it computes probabilities. It does not construct funnels; it identifies emergence. Conversion becomes not the result of persuasion, but the side effect of alignment between context, timing, and system intelligence.

This change has deep implications. It demands the abandonment of every legacy framework—funnels, personas, campaigns, linear journeys. It replaces them with a culture of hypothesis, iteration, and constant recalibration. Marketing ceases to be a map. It becomes a radar. The goal is not to lead the user somewhere, but to perceive where they already are.

The consequence is decisive: conversion is no longer a destination. It is an event—a transient one, measurable only when conditions align. Those who persist in thinking in terms of "journeys" will miss these events. They will create noise, speak too much, too late, and to the wrong people. They will not fail by incompetence, but by anachronism.

Those who learn to read patterns, on the other hand, will dominate silently. They will build systems that operate beneath awareness, precise yet invisible. They will be everywhere without being seen. Activated without being announced. This is the new marketing: a discipline that merges psychology, probability, and computation into one continuous process of behavioral alignment.

And this marketing will no longer speak to the client—it will accompany them. It will exist within their unconscious digital rhythm, within their pauses and impulses. Conversion will cease to be proof of persuasion; it will become a statistical artifact. And AI will stand as its invisible architect, orchestrating outcomes without ever needing to declare its presence.

Chapter 11 – The End of the Brand as a Benchmark

Introduction

For decades, the brand was seen as the central pillar of marketing. It embodied identity, conveyed meaning, and acted as a symbolic anchor in a noisy marketplace. A brand told a story, carried values, united communities, and inspired trust. Consumers projected emotion, belonging, and recognition onto it. Entire strategies were built around this symbolic capital: crafting logos, defining charters, repeating slogans, building awareness through emotional consistency. The brand was memory made visible. It gave form to loyalty and structure to desire.

That world is collapsing. The age of intelligent commerce—governed by artificial systems capable of anticipating and executing—has displaced the balance. Value no longer resides in the image projected by a company but in the trace it leaves. What matters is not what a brand promises, but what its systems can prove, measure, and verify. Users no longer need to choose consciously. They are served. They no longer express preference; they receive optimized results. It is no longer the brand that convinces—it is the system that triggers.

This transformation redefines the hierarchy of signals. Branding becomes peripheral. It no longer founds the decision; it does not even appear in the buying process. Behavioral data has taken control: purchase frequencies, satisfaction rates, return ratios, logistics efficiency, consistency of service. All these parameters feed the models that decide which product appears, which one disappears. Visibility no longer depends on a logo, but on algorithmic imprint. A brand can be admired yet forgotten, famous yet invisible, iconic yet absent from the flows that truly matter.

This chapter demonstrates that the value of a business no longer lies in what it claims, but in what it leaves behind. The trace replaces the symbol. The imprint replaces the identity. And in this new ecosystem, the brand no longer leads—it merely leaves evidence.

11.1 – The End of Branding as a Conscious Act

Building a brand was once the heart of every marketing strategy. It was a deliberate, structured process designed to create a mental identity—clear, memorable, differentiated. Every logo, color, and word carried meaning: the embodiment of values, the transmission of promises, the installation of instant recognition. Brands fought to occupy the consumer's mind, hoping to anchor themselves there through repetition, emotion, and storytelling. This framework rested on a single assumption: that the client's choice was conscious, that preference could be shaped through persuasion. Branding was a conquest of attention.

In the environment of intelligent commerce, that logic disintegrates. The consumer no longer chooses—he interacts. He responds. He follows algorithmic nudges, triggers contextual actions, receives optimized suggestions. He no longer wanders through a world of brands; he flows through a stream of solutions. What was once a conscious act of selection becomes an automated act of satisfaction. Branding loses its status as a strategic foundation and becomes a secondary feature, sometimes even invisible.

Artificial intelligence does not see logos. It does not interpret graphic charters. It is not moved by slogans. It processes behavioral signals, performance data, satisfaction patterns. In this context, branding no longer precedes the customer relationship; it follows it. It becomes a by-product of use, not a precursor of trust. What matters is not what the brand says, but what it enables—how it reduces friction, optimizes flow, delivers consistency. Consumption is detached from narrative dressing. The user is guided by efficiency, not identity.

Even loyalty has changed its nature. Consumers no longer return to a brand because they remember its promise, but because the system has flagged it as optimal in a given configuration. Loyalty becomes mechanical, functional. It emerges not from attachment, but from continuity of performance, minimal switching cost, or the inertia of an automated flow.

This does not mean brands no longer exist. It means they no longer trigger purchase. They survive in the background, as residual markers useful for rare exceptions—complex products, emotional decisions—but generally dissolved within algorithmic mediation. The brand, once the spearhead of conquest, becomes a side effect of data-driven relevance.

Power has shifted. Recommendation no longer belongs to the merchant or the brand but to the platforms and engines that mediate access to every market. They decide visibility. They dictate hierarchy. They erase identity markers in favor of pure efficiency. To exist, it is no longer enough to be loved. One must be legible to a machine.

This shift forces a total reallocation of marketing investment. Every dollar spent on communication must now be evaluated by its capacity to generate actionable traces—data points, behavioral signals, measurable feedback. Storytelling is no longer strategic capital; it is historical ornament. Perceived efficiency is no longer built on emotion, but on quantifiable reliability. Branding does not die. It becomes silent—absorbed into the system.

11.2 – Reputation: The New Algorithmic Currency

Reputation is no longer a human construct. It is no longer an image shaped by storytelling, nor a perception nurtured through campaigns, publicity, or word of mouth. It is no longer the fragile yet precious outcome of emotional trust between a brand and its customers. In the environment of AI-driven commerce, reputation has been translated, absorbed, and converted into a mathematical variable. It has become a statistical signal—a performance index derived from behavioral traces, weighted by consistency, reliability, and transactional coherence.

Intelligent systems that filter, rank, recommend, and decide do not need to be persuaded. They have no emotion, no opinion, no loyalty. They have data. And those data points now constitute reputation: return rates, delivery accuracy, repeat purchases, product coherence, after-sales responsiveness, claim frequency, customer satisfaction over time. Each element contributes to a behavioral graph—an invisible infrastructure of credibility. It does not exist to convince the consumer. It exists to guide the algorithm. And that guidance shapes the world: determining what is displayed, what is suggested, what is reachable. What the algorithm does not see, does not exist.

Thus, the company no longer speaks to its customers. It speaks to the architecture that connects them. It no longer communicates promises. It inscribes performance. It no longer nurtures mental images. It reinforces a score. That score is not symbolic; it is operational. It is used to estimate, predict, and recommend. It is not built to be admired—it is built to be computed.

This reconfiguration forces a brutal realignment of priorities. Every operational failure, even brief, carries an algorithmic cost. A late delivery, an unanticipated stock-out, a flawed product description, a delayed support response—all immediately degrade the score. These are no longer isolated incidents; they are statistical anomalies that reduce the probability of being recommended. And that probability has become the new battlefield. It is no longer visibility that sells, but integration within the flow. No longer marketing presence, but algorithmic persistence.

Campaigns, in this reality, lose their strategic sense. Influence becomes ineffective if it does not alter behavior. A marketing budget is wasted if it does not reinforce usable signals. Advertising is replaced by coherence. Discourse is replaced by performance. Opinion is replaced by data. The reputation of tomorrow is not an emotional halo—it is an index of consistency calculated by an indifferent machine.

And once established, this index becomes self-reinforcing. Systems are conservative: they learn from the past, they favor stability, they remember errors. Recovering from a penalty is not a matter of image management—it is a matter of reprogramming trust over thousands of verified interactions. A single deviation can take months to erase, if it ever disappears at all.

Algorithmic reputation is thus both an asset and a liability. Every deviation widens the gap between human satisfaction and machinic judgment. The customer may be happy, yet the system may not recommend. A problem may be solved, yet the trace remains. The machine does not forgive; it recalculates. And in this recalculation, intention carries no weight—only recurrence does.

Businesses must therefore redirect their investments. Emotional marketing loses priority to operational precision, transactional quality, and behavioral traceability. Branding becomes a residual effect. Reputation becomes a strategic input. It determines access to the customer—not because the customer wills it, but because the system grants it.

11.3 – The Trust of Machines

Trust used to be a human affair—a fragile equilibrium built through repeated positive interactions, transparency, and fulfilled promises.

Companies cultivated it through testimonials, guarantees, certifications, and loyalty programs. Trust was emotion stabilized by repetition. It was the emotional infrastructure of commerce.

But in the age of intelligent systems, the agent of trust has changed. The one who decides is no longer the human—it is the machine. Search engines, recommendation systems, voice assistants, and chatbots are the new intermediaries. They filter, classify, and prioritize. They connect needs to solutions. Users no longer seek— they delegate. They expect relevance, not persuasion. And they get it, without knowing the criteria behind it. They trust the interface by default, not by evaluation.

For the machine, trust is not belief—it is calculation. It has no empathy, no intuition, no memory of intention. It operates through probabilistic coherence. It cross-references transaction data, delivery stability, complaint ratios, usage frequencies, and satisfaction metrics. From this, it builds a relational graph of reliability. A company becomes "trustworthy" not because it tells the truth, but because it repeatedly aligns with predicted outcomes.

This redefines the very mechanics of competition. Emotional credibility loses ground to algorithmic precision. The brand that performs consistently is ranked higher, surfaced more often, and delivered faster. It wins not by narrative, but by statistical proof. A system that performs flawlessly is rewarded with visibility. One that falters disappears, not because people stop believing in it, but because the machine stops suggesting it.

To build this new kind of trust, companies must document everything. Every transaction, every delivery, every resolution must be traceable, interpretable, and machine-readable. Transparency no longer means honesty—it means structured data. Every inconsistency becomes a defect in the model. Every anomaly, a decline in the trust coefficient. Every silence, a missing input.

The relationship between companies and their markets is no longer direct. It is mediated by architectures that think and decide. The enterprise no longer speaks to a person—it speaks to an interpreter. And that interpreter, devoid of emotion, will only act upon quantifiable reliability. The conquest of algorithmic trust thus demands excellence that is not expressive but measurable.

In this logic, words no longer matter—only signals do. The new trust is not earned through persuasion. It is encoded through precision. The gaze of the client no longer decides. The equation does.

11.4 – The Forgetting of Brands

One of the most discreet yet radical shifts in intelligent commerce is the silent disappearance of brands from human memory. This is not a rejection, nor a crisis of confidence. It is something subtler: a structural amnesia. The user does not stop buying branded products—he simply stops remembering them. The mechanism is neither emotional nor ideological. It is functional. The user no longer needs to remember, because the system remembers for him.

The more predictive and automated the interfaces become, the less they require conscious recall. In a voice interface, one no longer says "I want Brand X shampoo." One says, "I need shampoo." The assistant interprets. It considers dozens of variables—price, performance, delivery time, satisfaction rate, context, stock proximity—and returns the most relevant product, not the most recognized. The user accepts, without thinking. Convenience replaces awareness. The act of delegation erases the act of remembrance.

In this architecture, the brand ceases to be evoked, cited, or even noticed. It operates beneath the surface, performing its function without narrative. The user is satisfied, yet indifferent. He no longer attributes his satisfaction to a logo or a name. The product worked;

that is enough. He moves on, ready to let the same invisible process repeat itself. The brand becomes operational rather than emotional—a component of the system, not of memory.

This quiet erasure profoundly undermines traditional marketing logic. For over a century, branding was about occupying mental space—engraving a name into consciousness through repetition, storytelling, design, and ritual. Every campaign, every jingle, every advertisement was a battle for mnemonic territory. But the modern consumer's cognitive field is now mediated by algorithms. The path between intention and action bypasses consciousness altogether. There is no longer a mental arena to conquer. The decision is pre-filtered, pre-ranked, pre-executed.

The result is paradoxical. The more efficient a brand becomes within intelligent systems, the more forgettable it grows in the human mind. The more seamlessly it performs, the less visible it is. The smoother the process, the less space it occupies in awareness. Success equals disappearance. Visibility becomes friction. Memory becomes irrelevant.

Some companies attempt to resist this erosion by amplifying creative storytelling—grand campaigns, bold imagery, emotional narratives. But these gestures fail to touch the true decision-maker. They appeal to humans while the system remains unmoved. They speak the wrong language. They produce beauty in a world that now responds only to precision.

The survival of a brand in such a world does not depend on visibility but on interpretability. The question is no longer, "Do people remember me?" but "Can the system understand me?" Optimization replaces persuasion. Alignment replaces affection. The winning brands will not be the most loved, but the most readable—those whose products, data, and structures are perfectly legible to algorithms.

In this new order, the brand becomes a by-product of efficiency. It is no longer invoked but integrated. It does not compete for memory; it competes for system access. Failure to align with algorithmic criteria does not result in scandal or rejection. It results in disappearance. The brand fades not with noise, but with silence. It is not defeated— it is simply no longer relevant.

11.5 – Conclusion: From Image to Imprint

For generations, marketing revolved around the worship of image. Brand image, perceived image, projected image. Everything was built on representation—communication, emotion, and aesthetic identity. The goal was to etch meaning into collective memory, to inspire attachment and recognition. Campaigns sought visibility, recall, affection. Success was measured in awareness, preference, and share of voice. Image mattered because attention was the currency.

That economy of attention no longer dominates. Automated recommendations, predictive systems, and invisible decision chains have displaced the logic of perception with the logic of computation. Purchase decisions are no longer made in the field of consciousness but within data flows. It is no longer stories that determine selection, but signals. It is no longer meaning that drives choice, but measured reliability. The image persists—but as a surface artifact. It may still seduce, but it no longer decides.

In the world of intelligent commerce, what matters is not what a brand shows, but what it leaves. Not visibility, but traceability. Not promise, but proof. Not recognition, but selection. The systems that now govern commerce remember differently. They do not store images; they store patterns. They do not retain emotion; they retain performance. They do not recall slogans; they calculate behaviors.

The brand's true capital becomes its algorithmic footprint—the cumulative record of its consistency, its precision, its reliability. Every delivery, every response, every transaction feeds this invisible score. This score determines ranking, visibility, and recommendation frequency. The brand no longer shines—it performs. Its equity is mathematical, not emotional.

This demands a profound strategic inversion. Communication must now serve operational truth. Marketing cannot be separated from performance. To be credible, one must be measurable. To be desired, one must be consistent. To endure, one must be interpretable. Creativity alone cannot sustain visibility. Rigor must now sustain presence.

Those who continue to invest solely in imagery will remain loved but unpurchased—remembered but unseen. Affection is no longer the driver of commerce; fluency is. Precision, not poetry, governs selection. Reliability, not storytelling, earns access. The future of marketing is not a war of narratives but a competition of signals.

The brands that master their algorithmic imprint will dominate quietly. They will not need to shout, because the system will choose them. Not out of love, but out of logic. They will win not by emotion, but by inevitability. The brand of tomorrow is not a name. It is a pattern of excellence—engraved not in minds, but in machines.

Chapter 12 – The End of User Experience

Introduction

User experience has long been the sacred center of digital design and marketing. Entire teams were devoted to improving interface fluidity, reducing friction, guiding users toward conversion, optimizing navigation, and maximizing perceived satisfaction. UX became both science and mantra—an ideology of empathy and control. Designers mapped user journeys, conducted tests, and refined micro-interactions to delight a supposedly active, conscious participant in his digital experience.

But that paradigm has expired. Not because it failed, but because the actor it was built around—the conscious user—has disappeared. Intelligent commerce no longer depends on interaction between a person and an interface. It depends on silent delegation to a system that acts on the person's behalf. The "experience" is no longer a journey; it is a result. No longer a navigation, but a prediction. Not a seduction, but an execution. The user no longer lives the experience; he inherits it.

In this new order, intention is no longer expressed; it is inferred. The click is replaced by suggestion. Exploration gives way to automation. Decision becomes recommendation. The interface dissolves. Cognitive effort disappears. The user no longer chooses—he is served, sometimes without even realizing it. The UX paradigm, designed for consciousness, yields to the AI/UX paradigm, designed for prediction. It is not about making interaction pleasant—it is about making it unnecessary.

This shift demands a total inversion of design philosophy. It is no longer about creating delightful paths but about guaranteeing invisible execution. No longer about guiding the user, but about acting for him. The designer's task is not to decorate a process but to remove it. The most elegant experience is not the one that captivates, but the one that never appears.

12.1 – When the Interface Disappears

The history of digital evolution has always been told through its interfaces. Each stage—command lines, graphical interfaces, websites, mobile apps, voice assistants—marked progress in accessibility. The interface was the bridge between human cognition and machine logic. The more natural and intuitive it became, the closer we felt to technology. UX was the pinnacle of this ambition: to make machines humanly legible. Designers learned to sculpt attention, to guide vision, to choreograph emotion through pixels and gestures.

But this entire framework rested on a hidden assumption—that humans would remain central to the process. Artificial intelligence breaks that assumption. Users no longer act; they delegate. They no longer enter systems; they expect systems to anticipate them. The interface, in this context, becomes redundant. It is a relic of an age when interaction was necessary. In the intelligent economy, the ideal interface is none at all.

The pioneers have already understood this. Amazon's Dash Buttons removed the website; Alexa removed the button. Google Assistant and Siri replaced search bars with conversation, and even conversation is now disappearing—replaced by anticipatory execution. The most successful systems are those the user never touches. In these architectures, the interface is not a design object but a symptom of failure: if a human still needs to click, the machine has not yet learned enough.

This is not the death of design, but its transformation. The designer's material is no longer the visual layout—it is the decision model. The goal is not to please the human eye but to optimize the system's response timing. Design moves from aesthetics to precision, from composition to correlation. What matters is not what appears on the screen, but what happens before the screen exists.

In this world, the user ceases to be the protagonist. He becomes the beneficiary of an invisible process. He no longer navigates; he is navigated for. The interface becomes a residual surface—a passing moment between two machine decisions. The real stage of commerce is no longer the page or the app, but the background computation that precedes them. The true experience happens upstream, in data flows and predictive engines.

The ultimate goal is not interaction—it is elimination. The disappearance of the interface is not a design failure; it is the logical endpoint of efficiency. Technology matures when it vanishes. The most advanced system is not the one that engages the user, but the one that no longer needs him.

12.2 – From Experience to Prediction

Traditional user experience relied on explicit action. The user signaled intention—searching, clicking, selecting, confirming. Systems responded. The design challenge was to make that dance effortless, beautiful, human. Engagement was measured in time spent, pages viewed, actions completed. The user's activity defined value.

Artificial intelligence overturns this choreography. It does not wait for intention—it anticipates it. It does not optimize clicks—it removes them. The goal is no longer to improve experience, but to bypass it. The user's agency is no longer required; his data suffice. Every pattern, hesitation, and micro-signal becomes a clue in the predictive chain. The machine acts before the human decides.

This makes the very notion of "experience" obsolete. When decisions are made upstream, there is no path to travel, no reflection to accompany, no moment to design. What we used to call "user experience" becomes a statistical outcome—a by-product of successful prediction. The best UX is not the one that feels intuitive; it is the one that does not need to exist.

Designers and marketers must therefore change their roles entirely. They are no longer architects of journeys but engineers of accuracy. They no longer craft messages but calibrate reactions. They no longer analyze personas but model probabilities. The success of a design is no longer measured by delight, but by the absence of interaction. A click becomes a symptom of inefficiency. A page view, a sign of lag. A scroll, an admission that the system did not anticipate enough.

Measurement itself must evolve. Old KPIs—bounce rate, dwell time, conversion funnels—lose relevance. What matters is not what users do, but what they do not need to do. Efficiency is measured in avoided effort, in correctly predicted outcomes, in the invisibility of friction. The new satisfaction metric is silence.

Companies that understand this shift are already reorganizing. UX teams merge with data science. Designers learn machine learning. Product managers study predictive modeling. The craft of persuasion becomes the science of precision. The emotional bond between user and interface fades; what remains is functional dependency. The brand that anticipates becomes indispensable. The one that waits becomes irrelevant.

The user of the past wanted to choose. The user of the present wants to be relieved of choice. The UX of the future will no longer be designed for him—it will be designed for the machine that chooses for him.

12.3 – Toward AI/UX: Designing for the Assistant, Not the Human

The most profound and least discussed evolution in digital design concerns its true audience. For decades, we designed for the human user. Every pixel, every motion, every sound cue was meant to appeal to perception, emotion, comprehension. Designers crafted experiences to help humans understand systems. Today, that relationship is reversed. It is no longer humans who must understand systems. It is systems that must understand humans. And the bridge between the two is no longer visual—it is algorithmic.

In the age of intelligent commerce, the human client is no longer the primary interlocutor. The real client is his digital proxy: the assistant, the algorithmic agent, the autonomous recommender that acts in his name. This proxy is immune to persuasion. It has no preferences, no moods, no emotions. It processes parameters—price, delay, satisfaction rate, energy cost, compliance level, historical reliability. It negotiates without empathy. It chooses without narrative. And it does so millions of times per second.

For a company, this means the old craft of UX must mutate into something radically different: AI/UX, the art of designing for intelligibility, not seduction. The system no longer needs to look beautiful. It needs to be legible—to machines. Every product, every service, every process must be structured, standardized, and interpretable by algorithms. The vocabulary of design changes: from interface to data schema, from layout to ontology, from animation to metadata.

Aesthetics gives way to semantics. Where the designer once arranged color and form, he must now organize taxonomies and descriptors. Where marketers once built messages, they must now define fields and formats. Every piece of content becomes an input for an algorithmic negotiation. Every attribute—a product dimension, a delivery window, a return rate—feeds the decision graph of an assistant that will never read the brand's manifesto or admire its visual identity.

Consider a simple case: a corporate assistant automatically reorders printer supplies. It does not browse websites. It does not read ads. It does not watch videos. It queries APIs. It evaluates data quality, delivery reliability, and conformity to specification. A missing field in a JSON response can outweigh a million euros of brand image. What matters is not persuasion—it is precision.

This redesign of commerce imposes a tectonic shift in corporate culture. Creativity must collaborate with engineering. Designers must work with data scientists. Marketing directors must speak the language of protocol and model evaluation. The distinction between creative and technical teams collapses. The company's success depends on how clearly its systems communicate with other systems.

In this environment, "experience" no longer means how humans feel—it means how machines interpret. The new design principles are reliability, predictability, and interpretability. The question is no longer "does it look good?" but "can it be parsed?" The best-designed product is not the one that delights a customer, but the one that an assistant always selects.

The transition from UX to AI/UX marks the final abstraction of marketing. It is no longer the dialogue between a seller and a buyer—it is the negotiation between two models. Humans remain involved, but their influence fades. The commercial frontier moves deeper into the realm of machine logic, where design becomes code and persuasion becomes computation.

12.4 – Conclusion: An UX Without a User

User experience, once the cornerstone of digital design, was built around a simple conviction: the user must be at the center. Everything—from interface layouts to service flows—was designed to make human interaction effortless and enjoyable. But that conviction no longer matches reality. The user, as an active decision-maker, has been quietly removed from the loop.

The interface, once the altar of interaction, is now a ghost layer. The real exchanges take place elsewhere—in data flows, predictive models, and orchestration engines. The experience is not lived; it is executed. The user does not navigate; he is navigated. He does not decide; he confirms—or, more often, he is bypassed. The notion of an intentional, aware, choosing subject has been replaced by that of a modeled, anticipated, and served entity.

In this new logic, the object of design shifts from attraction to executability. The challenge is no longer to seduce the eye, but to ensure operational consistency across invisible systems. A successful experience is not one that pleases—it is one that works. The highest compliment a user can pay is not delight, but indifference: the system functioned so perfectly that he never noticed it.

This is not simplification. It is complexity hidden behind apparent simplicity. Beneath every seamless action lies a dense architecture of prediction models, feedback loops, and optimization protocols. The company that survives in this ecosystem is not the one that tells the best story, but the one that leaves the cleanest trace. Every process must be measurable, every action interpretable, every event traceable. What cannot be read cannot be recommended. What cannot be measured cannot exist.

The marketer's vocabulary must evolve. "Interface" becomes "integration." "Design" becomes "interpretation." "Experience" becomes "execution." The only remaining aesthetic is the elegance of efficiency. Brands that continue to invest in visible UX without optimizing for machine readability will vanish from the algorithmic landscape—not because users reject them, but because systems ignore them.

The ethical frontier of design now lies in truth and clarity. The new elegance is transparency. Manipulation of attention is obsolete; orchestration of trust is essential. Companies must design not for emotion, but for coherence. They must ensure their actions can be understood, weighted, and transmitted across systems. The user no longer judges. The machine does.

The end of user experience is not the end of design. It is its transcendence. The interface dissolves, but design remains— migrated into the invisible. The new designer shapes not pixels, but probabilities. He no longer decorates the surface of technology—he structures its logic. The user, meanwhile, no longer experiences the brand. He experiences the result.

The UX is dead.
What replaces it no longer needs a user.

Chapter 13 – The End of the Art of Marketing

Introduction

Marketing was once celebrated as the most creative discipline of capitalism—the art of understanding desires, shaping needs, and telling stories that would connect brands to their audiences. It was a blend of psychology, intuition, and persuasion: a craft that turned attention into emotion, and emotion into action. But that art form is fading.

What we called marketing belonged to an age when visibility was power and the human mind was the battlefield. Strategies revolved around the message—what to say, how to say it, and to whom. Campaigns were built like theatrical productions, complete with audiences, scripts, and applause. The marketer was both storyteller and strategist, weaving meaning to capture loyalty.

Artificial intelligence has rewritten that playbook. The economy of emotion has given way to the economy of precision. The customer is no longer a listener; he is a dataset. The message is no longer a story; it is a variable. The act of persuasion has been replaced by the act of activation. The "art" of marketing is not dying because creativity has vanished—it is dying because the structure of decision-making itself has changed.

In this new order, marketing ceases to be expressive. It becomes infrastructural. It does not speak—it calibrates. It no longer paints in colors of emotion—it codes in probabilities of action. The campaign gives way to the context. The creative brief gives way to the learning loop. Marketing becomes invisible, embedded, algorithmic. What was once a stage has become a system.

13.1 – From Message to Environment

Traditional marketing was built on a clear linear model: sender, message, medium, receiver. The company crafted a message, chose a channel, targeted an audience, and waited for a response. The efficiency of the process was measured in visibility, recall, and conversion. It was a logic of diffusion: to influence, one had to be heard.

But that model assumes something that no longer exists—an attentive, available consumer, open to persuasion. Today's individual is overwhelmed by signals, notifications, and stimuli. His attention is not a resource to capture; it is an anomaly to respect. The message has lost its place of privilege. In its stead stands the environment—a network of contexts in which behavior occurs naturally, without explicit invitation or conscious decision.

The environment is not a campaign. It is a configuration. It merges timing, relevance, convenience, and trust into a self-evident proposal. The customer no longer reads or listens; he reacts—or better, he is triggered. The best marketing message is the one that never needs to be sent, because the conditions for action have already been met.

This shift transforms the marketer from storyteller to architect. The new task is not to tell a brand's truth but to design the environment where its truth becomes inevitable. Marketing becomes spatial rather than narrative, situational rather than declarative. Instead of pushing information outward, it configures a landscape where every interaction is pre-optimized.

The KPIs evolve accordingly. Impressions, reach, and awareness give way to friction scores, latency indices, and contextual relevance metrics. The objective is no longer persuasion—it is predictability. The measure of success is not whether the audience listens, but whether the environment behaves.

This is not a loss of creativity—it is its relocation. The canvas is no longer the billboard or the feed; it is the ecosystem. The creative act lies in arranging data, interfaces, and triggers so precisely that buying becomes the path of least resistance. In this logic, the message itself becomes noise. True influence is silent.

13.2 – The Orchestration of Weak Signals

Classical marketing segmented reality into neat typologies: age, income, geography, lifestyle. It spoke to "targets" and "personas," archetypes that simplified complexity. But such segmentation was a comfortable illusion. It treated humans as averages, not as dynamic organisms.

Artificial intelligence shattered that simplification. It does not divide—it correlates. It does not assume—it observes. It reads the infinitesimal: a pause, a hesitation, a recurrent behavior, a deviation from pattern. It listens not to what users declare, but to what their micro-actions reveal. Each gesture, however trivial, becomes a clue. Each moment becomes a probability field.

Marketing, in this world, no longer operates by plan but by orchestration. The marketer is not a scheduler of campaigns but a conductor of signals. He does not dictate; he harmonizes. He sets parameters and lets systems adapt. He does not imagine the consumer's mind; he monitors the system's responses. The job is no longer to persuade, but to synchronize.

This orchestration is continuous. The system learns from every reaction, updating models in real time, refining its sense of what matters. A campaign once required months of planning and post-analysis. The new marketing executes thousands of micro-adjustments per second. It replaces the fiction of foresight with the reality of feedback.

What emerges is a living, breathing structure—a Darwinian marketplace of ideas and actions. Strategies evolve organically, not by decree but by performance. The algorithms keep only what works, discard what fails, and replicate the rest across every channel. There is no longer a "launch." There is only learning.

The marketer's creativity, once externalized in slogans and visuals, now expresses itself in logic and architecture. The art is no longer in telling the story—it is in making the system capable of telling itself, differently, for every user, every time.

13.3 – The End of Campaigns

The very word "campaign" implies rhythm, beginning, end, climax, and rest—a linear narrative that assumes stable audiences and controlled timing. But the intelligent economy has no seasons. It flows. There is no start or finish, no target, no pause. Every user exists in a unique temporal micro-context, every signal evolves in real time.

To "launch" a campaign in such a world is to interrupt a system that already functions. It introduces friction, redundancy, and noise. AI does not campaign—it listens. It reacts continuously, not episodically. It is a perpetual presence, not a scheduled event.

In this logic, the campaign becomes an anachronism. It is too heavy, too slow, too human. Its theatricality belongs to an era of broadcasting, not computation. The intelligent system does not need to shout—it needs to respond. Marketing becomes an unending flow of micro-adaptations, invisible to the eye but omnipresent in effect.

This demands a cultural revolution. The creative calendar dissolves. The brief becomes a dataset. The marketing department merges with engineering. The ad agency becomes an API. The question is no longer "what do we say?" but "how do we learn?" There are no more audiences—only contexts. No more launches—only loops.

In the age of automation, the true campaign is the absence of one. The brand that never stops learning, adjusting, predicting, and responding will outperform the one that still waits for approval to speak.

13.4 – Marketing Becomes a Backend

Marketing used to be the face of business. It smiled, seduced, and spoke in slogans. It lived on the surface—visible, loud, theatrical. But its new home is behind the scenes. Marketing has become infrastructure. It no longer tells stories; it enables them. It no longer addresses humans; it coordinates machines.

Modern marketing is not a department—it is a layer of logic integrated into every process. It feeds data into recommendation engines, powers chatbots, tunes pricing models, and orchestrates customer flows. It no longer produces assets but generates parameters. It no longer broadcasts messages but configures triggers.

In this world, the Chief Marketing Officer resembles a systems architect more than a creative director. He must understand data pipelines, feedback loops, and interoperability. He must collaborate with engineers, AI specialists, and analysts. His canvas is not Photoshop—it is the API documentation.

The distinction between marketing and product collapses. Between marketing and logistics, between marketing and analytics. The discipline no longer promotes—it permeates. It operates as an internal nervous system that connects the sensory and motor functions of the enterprise.

The beauty of this invisible marketing lies in its precision. It requires no applause, no visibility, no recognition. It measures success not by attention captured but by friction removed. The best marketing strategy is one that the user never notices because it functions so seamlessly that it feels like nature.

13.5 – Conclusion: Marketing Without Marketing

What we once called marketing was a spectacle. It relied on visibility, emotion, and persuasion. It needed audiences and applause. But in the era of intelligent commerce, it has become a system of synchronization.

The art of marketing has not died—it has migrated underground. It no longer paints messages; it sculpts behavior. It no longer seeks attention; it ensures inevitability. The marketer's new mission is not to convince, but to configure. Not to shine, but to function.

The companies that cling to the old art will continue to speak beautifully—to no one. Their creativity will echo in empty spaces. Meanwhile, those who understand that marketing is now a backend discipline—a silent logic embedded in every process—will dominate quietly.

The new marketing does not need a campaign. It does not need an audience. It does not even need a name. It is the hidden architecture of relevance—the invisible algorithm that ensures that what must happen, happens.

The art is gone.
The system remains.

Chapter 14 – The Business Model Is Obsolete

Introduction

For decades, the architecture of entrepreneurship relied on the stability of a business model. Finding the right formula was the ultimate goal: identifying a target segment, defining a clear value proposition, creating an efficient distribution chain, optimizing a coherent pricing strategy, and forecasting a trajectory of profitability over time. The model provided comfort and structure. It reassured investors and offered entrepreneurs a sense of control in a world still governed by relatively predictable dynamics. The business model was seen as the backbone of the company—a strategic compass that organized every operational decision.

But that paradigm has collapsed. The very idea of a fixed model has become incompatible with a world governed by artificial intelligence. Consumer behavior is no longer linear. Attention cycles shorten to seconds. Technological ecosystems evolve faster than any strategic plan can adapt. Platforms rewrite the rules without warning, and intermediaries emerge and vanish at a pace that makes long-term modeling absurd. The business model once assumed a form of predictability—but predictability itself has disappeared.

In this new landscape, it is not the model that determines resilience but adaptability. What defines a company's strength is no longer its ability to execute a plan, but its ability to learn continuously. To capture weak signals. To test, iterate, and pivot before the market does. Value has migrated from the structure to the mechanism— from the model to the capacity to evolve. The competitive advantage no longer lies in what a company knows but in how fast it can unlearn.

To survive, companies must evolve from a model-based to an ecosystem-based mindset. They must be conceived not as static entities but as living organisms—structures capable of sensing, learning, and transforming themselves. In this logic, the business plan is no longer a prediction but a hypothesis, always temporary, always under revision. Data becomes the circulatory system of this organism, transforming every interaction into actionable intelligence.

This transformation is not a simple adjustment. It is a revolution. The entrepreneur's task is no longer to design a perfect model but to build the conditions for continuous intelligent mutation. Stability has become a liability. Rigid execution is now a risk. The business model, once a strategic certainty, has become a transient configuration—one that must dissolve as soon as it ceases to create learning.

The age of fixed models is over. What determines longevity is not the ability to optimize a structure but to reconfigure it endlessly. Success now depends on transforming uncertainty into a strategic resource—on orchestrating instability instead of resisting it. The strongest companies do not have models. They have loops—self-improving, self-learning mechanisms of adaptation that turn every disruption into an opportunity. This is the essence of the learning ecosystem: a structure without form but with direction, without rigidity but with purpose.

14.1 – The End of Static Modeling

Traditional business models were designed as elegant, predictable structures intended to map economic reality. They defined customer segments, value propositions, revenue sources, and cost frameworks. On paper, they offered logic, coherence, and reassurance. But in the era of intelligent commerce, this static logic has become a liability. It freezes organizations in a world that no longer stays still.

The flaw is not in the model itself but in believing that it can remain valid. The world no longer operates within stable boundaries. Consumer behaviors shift without notice. Channels fragment. Algorithms redefine visibility overnight. Pricing structures implode under the weight of automation. The environment that once allowed models to hold has dissolved into continuous volatility. In such a context, a fixed model is not security—it is paralysis.

Every assumption underpinning static modeling has been invalidated. What worked yesterday may fail tomorrow. What was profitable in one version of the market collapses in the next. What guaranteed stability can vanish with a software update or a platform change. The economy has become probabilistic, and linear frameworks are incompatible with probability.

The age of intelligent commerce demands a new temporal logic: real-time adaptability. Companies no longer need business models—they need feedback loops. They must replace planning with continuous experimentation, prediction with observation, and long-term certainty with dynamic hypotheses. The model becomes a tool for testing, not a structure to defend. Its validity lies only in its ability to evolve faster than its obsolescence.

This shift requires founders to abandon the quest for the "right" model. There is no formula—only systems capable of generating new models on demand. Value is no longer in the plan but in the reflex: the capacity to perceive weak signals, to interpret anomalies, to transform friction into innovation. The company becomes an engine of adaptation, not a follower of frameworks.

Every variable must be negotiable. Pricing must adjust fluidly. Channels must be replaceable. Propositions must evolve with context. Customer segments must expand and contract dynamically. Nothing is sacred except adaptability itself. True resilience comes from embedding instability into the DNA of the organization.

The companies that cling to rigid models will not collapse because they lack ambition, but because they mistake precision for permanence. They optimize plans that are already outdated. They build cathedrals of logic on foundations of shifting sand. Intelligent commerce requires the opposite: structures that breathe, evolve, and self-correct in motion.

The goal is no longer efficiency but plasticity. It is not about being right—it is about being ready. Strategy becomes a dynamic system of hypotheses. Management becomes orchestration. Leadership becomes the art of unlearning. The winners will not be those with the best model, but those capable of changing models faster than the world changes rules.

14.2 – The Company as an Experimentation Engine

In the industrial paradigm, companies were machines designed to execute a plan. A product was developed, launched, and optimized according to a predefined roadmap. The entire organization revolved around stability: stable demand, stable competition, stable processes. Once validated, a model was to be repeated indefinitely. Success depended on discipline, not discovery.

That logic no longer works. The intelligent economy rewards adaptability, not execution. Markets now evolve faster than strategies can be formalized. In this world, a company's strength lies in its ability to experiment—continuously, intelligently, and collectively. Experimentation is no longer a phase within innovation. It is the structure of innovation itself.

The experimental company treats every action as a hypothesis. Every campaign, product, and feature is a test designed to generate feedback. Nothing is final. The organization learns by doing, adjusting, and iterating in real time. The goal is not perfection but evolution. The company becomes a living laboratory—one where learning loops replace hierarchies and adaptability replaces authority.

Artificial intelligence amplifies this approach. It accelerates learning cycles, detects anomalies, automates testing, and measures outcomes instantly. But AI also introduces a dependency: it must be fed with relevant data. Without continuous experimentation, the system stagnates. Without structured failure, there is no improvement. Blind organizations are not those that make mistakes—they are those that stop testing.

The CEO of an experimental company no longer approves plans; they design environments where hypotheses can live or die quickly. Testing becomes inexpensive, frequent, and expected. Failure is not punished—it is processed. This demands a new culture: curiosity over control, adaptability over efficiency, evolution over optimization.

This is not chaos. It is disciplined fluidity. It demands precise measurement, transparent documentation, and continuous feedback loops. It requires systems that remember, learn, and adapt at every iteration. It transforms management into orchestration and replaces strategic rigidity with adaptive intelligence.

This also changes the nature of talent. The most valuable employees are no longer those who follow procedures flawlessly but those who can design, test, and interpret experiments. The new professional archetype is not the executor—it is the experimenter, the adaptation engineer, the strategist in motion.

In this model, the business plan is not a starting point but an outcome—a temporary product of constant learning. Strategy is no longer a fixed statement but a self-correcting system. The company ceases to be a machine that produces; it becomes an organism that evolves. It stops asking, "What should we do next?" and starts asking, "What can we learn now?"

14.3 – Distributed Value

One of the deepest disruptions brought by algorithmic economics lies in the fragmentation of value creation. In the industrial model, value flowed linearly—from supplier to manufacturer to distributor to customer. Each link captured a share of profit. Control was vertical. The company owned its product, its distribution, and its customer relationship. That clarity has vanished.

In intelligent commerce, value is no longer produced along a chain but within a network. A product is no longer a static object transferred from one hand to another; it is a node within a system. Every transaction is the result of thousands of invisible micro-interactions: recommendation algorithms, logistics partners, payment gateways, reviews, data brokers. The merchant is no longer the sole creator of value—merely one contributor among many.

Take something as simple as a shampoo. It is no longer just a liquid in a bottle. It is a data point within a behavioral graph. It is contextualized by an algorithmic recommendation, delivered within hours by automated logistics, paid through predictive credit scoring, reviewed by an AI-moderated community, and re-purchased through a replenishment engine. Every actor in this chain—from the algorithm to the courier—captures a slice of the value generated.

The traditional business model, built on ownership, cannot function in this distributed reality. The goal is no longer to control every link but to orchestrate them. Success depends on how well a company integrates into networks, not on how tightly it owns them. The strongest advantage is no longer vertical control but horizontal connectivity.

To thrive, companies must evolve from proprietary to participatory thinking. They must open their systems, standardize their interfaces, and embrace interoperability. APIs become the new contracts. Data-sharing becomes the new partnership. Profit is shared, but so is learning. The goal is not to extract more value alone but to generate more value together.

This shift also changes how innovation happens. It is no longer the result of internal R&D but of collective iteration. Companies that open themselves to external contributions evolve faster. Ecosystems amplify intelligence. Innovation becomes a social process. The company ceases to be a fortress and becomes a platform.

In a distributed-value economy, traditional KPIs lose relevance. Profit margins say little about resilience. What matters is network centrality—the degree to which a company is indispensable to the system. Power lies not in owning the pipeline but in being the node through which everything passes.

14.4 – From Profitability to Resilience

For centuries, profitability was the ultimate measure of success. Every strategic decision, every investment, every process was evaluated through financial returns. Efficiency was the religion; ROI was the scripture. But in a world defined by volatility, uncertainty, and algorithmic speed, profitability alone becomes a weak compass. What matters now is resilience—the ability to absorb shocks, pivot rapidly, and adapt without breaking.

Resilience is strategic plasticity. It is the capacity to mutate under pressure, to learn from disruption, to rebuild in motion. In an era when markets shift quarterly and technologies monthly, a profitable but rigid company is fragile. A flexible company that learns faster than it fails will always survive longer.

Resilience demands abandoning short-term optimization in favor of long-term adaptability. It redefines performance indicators: the speed of reaction, the fluidity of resources, the modularity of systems. It values diversity, redundancy, and experimentation over linear efficiency. It treats uncertainty not as a threat but as raw material for evolution.

Data becomes the foundation of this resilience. Companies that do not measure, analyze, and interpret in real time are blind. But data alone is not enough—it must circulate freely across functions. Silos must disappear. Systems must interconnect. Architecture becomes strategy.

Resilience is also cultural. It depends on a workforce trained to learn, to question, to improvise. It values curiosity as much as competence, flexibility as much as expertise. It encourages testing, not compliance. The company that tolerates error is the company that survives change.

For investors and analysts, this shift demands new evaluation criteria. Financial ratios must give way to learning ratios—the ability to reallocate resources, implement new technologies, and reconfigure processes on demand. The resilient company is not the one performing best today but the one most capable of existing tomorrow.

14.5 – Conclusion: Thinking the Company as an Organism

We have spent too long conceiving the company as a machine—predictable, optimized, controllable. That worldview made sense in an industrial age built on repetition. But we now live in an organic age—fluid, chaotic, interdependent. Markets are not chains but ecosystems. Value is not produced but propagated. Stability is not strength but fragility.

To survive, a company must stop functioning like an engine and start behaving like an organism. It must sense, react, evolve, regenerate. It must abandon the fantasy of permanence and embrace the discipline of transformation. The goal is not to master the environment but to remain compatible with it.

An organism seeks dynamic balance, not immobility. It thrives not by control but by adaptability. It processes shocks, heals, mutates. It is modular by nature. It is governed by feedback loops, not hierarchies. This is the model of the intelligent enterprise—resilient, distributed, self-learning.

In such an organization, every structure must be designed for movement. Business models must be temporary. Tools must be replaceable. Leadership must be contextual. The only constant is the system's ability to reconfigure itself. The company's value lies not in its products or plans but in its metabolism.

The challenge for leaders is to accept this biological logic. To stop optimizing the machine and start cultivating the organism. To shift from control to orchestration, from prediction to sensing, from execution to evolution. The future does not belong to companies that resist change but to those that embody it.

The business model is no longer the foundation of the enterprise—it is its shadow. What endures is not the structure but the motion. The companies that survive will not be the strongest, nor the most profitable, but the most adaptable. Because in the age of intelligent commerce, survival itself has become an act of intelligence.

Chapter 15 – The Product Is No Longer the Value

Introduction

For centuries, the notion of "product" stood at the center of economic gravity. It was the anchor of every strategy, the object around which marketing, production, and distribution revolved. Companies built their identity through it, organized their factories around it, and measured their success by how many units they sold. The product embodied creativity, innovation, and profitability—it was the tangible proof of value creation.

But in the intelligent economy, that centrality is dissolving. The product has not disappeared; it has been absorbed. It no longer carries value by itself—it generates it through data. Its purpose is no longer to be used, but to be observed. In the era of artificial intelligence, the product becomes a sensor, a signal, a trigger. Its true function is to feed information into the system—information about context, usage, frequency, intention, satisfaction.

The logic of commerce has shifted from selling objects to processing signals. The shampoo, the phone, the coffee machine—each is now an interface between the physical world and a predictive model. What matters is not what the product does, but what it reveals about the one who uses it. The value no longer resides in the thing itself but in the insight it generates.

This inversion of perspective is not technological—it is philosophical. It changes how companies innovate, how they design, how they measure success. The R&D department is no longer a factory for features but a laboratory for behavioral understanding. A company that still believes its product is the core of its value misunderstands the nature of modern competition.

The product is no longer the end. It is the beginning—the entry point to a loop of learning, data collection, and predictive optimization. Those who grasp this shift stop selling things and start orchestrating knowledge. They stop building catalogues and start constructing systems. They stop thinking in units and start thinking in flows.

15.1 – The Commodification of the Signal

Every digital gesture produces a trace: a click, a pause, a hesitation, a search that does not end, a product added to a cart and abandoned, a delayed response to a notification, an unusual browsing path. Each of these micro-actions is a fragment of signal—a reflection of intention, attention, or distraction. In the traditional economy, these fragments were invisible. They evaporated. Today, they are the raw material of the intelligent economy.

Commerce is no longer the exchange of goods—it is the exchange of signals. What is sold is not the shampoo, but the understanding of who buys it, when, how, and why. Each interaction generates metadata: time, location, correlation, emotional state inferred from behavior. This metadata is infinitely more valuable than the object itself, because it accumulates, cross-references, and predicts.

In this world, the product becomes a vector of capture. It is no longer optimized for physical performance but for informational performance. It is designed to record as much as it cleans, connects, or entertains. Its purpose is to feed the system with structured and contextualized feedback—real-time insight that allows algorithms to learn faster than competitors can react.

The transaction itself is only a pretext for data acquisition. The more the product is used, the richer the model becomes. The more signals it emits, the smarter the system grows. Where the object once decayed through use, it now increases in value through interaction. The more it is consumed, the more it teaches.

This inversion transforms the very nature of economic exchange. The product is no longer the source of profit—the signal is. The shampoo becomes a data portal. The car becomes a mobile sensor. The phone becomes an extension of predictive infrastructure. The company sells not a function but an access point to an ecosystem of insight.

The commodification of the signal redefines ownership. The consumer no longer buys; they participate. Each gesture, each consent, each usage enriches a networked intelligence that belongs to no one—and to everyone who knows how to exploit it. The real capital is not inventory but information velocity. The market becomes a competition between systems that learn.

15.2 – Value Resides in Usage

In the old economy, value was captured at the moment of sale. The customer paid; the company recorded revenue; the relationship was complete. The post-purchase experience was anecdotal. What mattered was conversion. Once the transaction closed, the customer disappeared from the radar until the next campaign.

That logic is dead. In the data-driven economy, the transaction is the beginning, not the end. Value is generated through continuous usage, through interaction loops that feed learning systems. The sale no longer closes a relationship—it initiates one. The product is valuable not when it is bought, but when it is used, reused, connected, and contextualized.

Every repetition, every variation, every pause in usage generates new data. Each pattern teaches the system something: what triggers engagement, what causes abandonment, what drives loyalty. The company's intelligence grows not by selling more, but by understanding more. The key metric is no longer conversion but retention, not revenue but recurrence.

The product is no longer a one-time deliverable but a service node—a gateway into a dynamic experience. Subscription models, continuous updates, and predictive maintenance all stem from this logic. The product evolves, learns, personalizes itself through use. What is monetized is no longer ownership but participation.

This transformation forces companies to shift from a logic of selling to a logic of sustaining. They must design not for purchase but for permanence. The marketing department becomes a system of behavioral calibration. The objective is not to persuade once but to engage continuously—to transform each moment of use into a feedback loop.

In this paradigm, the product is no longer a commodity but a conduit. It lives through its user, and its value grows as long as that usage persists. The more the company learns from the user, the better it predicts the next move, the next need, the next context. It becomes less a manufacturer than an interpreter of behavior.

The economy of usage replaces the economy of sale. It rewards fluidity over finality. The product is no longer the object of the relationship—it is the medium of connection. What matters is not what the customer buys, but what the system learns from their continuous interaction.

15.3 – The Product as a Learning Infrastructure

In the traditional economy, the product was an endpoint—a finished object designed to deliver a stable function. Once produced and sold, it left the company's hands, inert and immutable. In the intelligent economy, the product becomes the opposite: an open, evolving infrastructure for learning. It is no longer built to last but to learn.

Every interaction with the product becomes an event in a data pipeline. Each action—activation, customization, replacement—feeds the company's central intelligence. The product's lifecycle is now a flow of information: production → usage → feedback → update → optimization → reproduction. The physical cycle mirrors a cognitive one.

To enable this, products must be designed differently. They need embedded sensors, connectivity, traceability, interoperability. They must generate structured data usable by the system in real time. Design no longer stops at ergonomics—it extends to data architecture. The form follows not function, but feedback.

This approach redefines R&D. Product teams no longer aim to deliver perfection; they aim to build learning nodes. The product is a probe, a testing instrument. It collects anomalies, detects preferences, maps invisible patterns. It transforms every user into an unwitting co-researcher.

An intelligent haircare product, for instance, is not just a shampoo. It becomes a feedback mechanism: identifying the user's environment, frequency, seasonality, satisfaction level. It captures data that can adjust recommendations, supply chains, or even formulas. The product thus becomes both the source and the recipient of learning.

The company that masters this loop stops designing products and starts designing systems of improvement. The competitive advantage becomes cumulative: each iteration strengthens the system, deepens its knowledge base, and enhances predictive precision. Unlike physical goods, knowledge compounds—it scales infinitely.

The product, then, is no longer a unit of production. It is a unit of intelligence. Its purpose is to extend the company's awareness into the real world. It is not manufactured to perform but to perceive. It becomes the sensory organ of the enterprise, connecting corporate logic to lived experience.

15.4 – The Datafication of the Enterprise

The rise of intelligent products is only one aspect of a broader metamorphosis: the datafication of the enterprise. Every action, every decision, every transaction becomes an event in an information system. The company ceases to be a collection of departments—it becomes an integrated network of sensors, processes, and models.

In the traditional company, data was a byproduct of activity—a reporting tool, used retrospectively to assess performance. In the datafied company, data is the activity itself. It is the bloodstream that sustains decision-making. It connects marketing to logistics, HR to finance, operations to strategy. Everything becomes measurable, correlatable, actionable.

This transformation dissolves hierarchies. Silos collapse as information flows horizontally across the organization. The supply chain becomes a self-adjusting organism. The marketing team no longer launches campaigns but triggers events. Finance stops projecting; it simulates. The company evolves from a bureaucratic machine into a real-time cognitive system.

To enable this, technology must be modular, scalable, and interoperable. The legacy ERP gives way to event-driven architectures, data lakes, and knowledge graphs. APIs replace middle management. The structure becomes software. The CEO becomes an orchestrator of flows rather than a controller of people.

But datafication is not just technical—it is cultural. It demands that organizations think probabilistically rather than deterministically. It requires comfort with ambiguity, willingness to experiment, and fluency in failure. Power no longer resides in seniority but in the ability to interpret complexity. Leadership becomes analytical empathy: understanding systems as living entities.

Traceability becomes universal. Every decision is logged, every process mapped, every error recorded. Far from being oppressive, this transparency allows collective learning. The organization develops memory—a consciousness of its own performance. Over time, it becomes self-aware.

The company's real value no longer lies in physical assets or human capital alone, but in informational capital: the richness, accuracy, and fluidity of its data. The smarter the infrastructure, the greater the strategic resilience. Intelligence becomes the ultimate intangible asset.

15.5 – Conclusion: To Produce Is to Capture

In the age of intelligent commerce, production is no longer the creation of objects but the creation of insights. To produce is to observe. To sell is to learn. Every act of manufacturing, every marketing campaign, every transaction is an opportunity to capture and refine information.

The purpose of production shifts from delivering functionality to generating feedback. A product that does not capture signals is incomplete. A process that does not generate learning is waste. The company that produces without perceiving is already behind.

The essence of commerce has changed. The factory is now a neural network. The product is a data conduit. The sale is a training event. The supply chain is a predictive graph. The customer is an input signal. Every element of the enterprise contributes to the same loop: sense, process, learn, improve.

Value no longer resides in the object, but in the knowledge accumulated around it. The company that learns faster than it sells will always outperform the one that sells faster than it learns.

To produce, in the intelligent economy, is to capture reality and transform it into predictive intelligence. The product is only a vessel. The real creation happens elsewhere—in the system that learns from it. The companies that understand this truth will not only survive the end of the product age. They will define what comes after it.

Chapter 16 – The Client Is Dead, Long Live the Behavioral Entity

Introduction

For more than a century, the figure of the "client" has been the central character in the theater of commerce. Everything revolved around him: strategies, products, communications, loyalty programs, market studies. The client was both the alpha and the omega—the subject to seduce, understand, and retain. Companies gave him a name, a face, an age, and a set of preferences. Marketing turned him into a persona, a rational actor guided by identifiable motivations. But that image, once foundational, has evaporated.

In the age of artificial intelligence, the client is no longer a person—it is a pattern. The system does not address identities but behaviors. It does not listen to intentions but observes gestures. It does not wait for answers—it infers probabilities. The human disappears behind the trace of his actions, reduced to a sequence of micro-events processed in real time. The "client" becomes a derived entity, a statistical shadow, a behavioral construct continuously recalculated and optimized.

This transformation is not metaphorical—it is operational. The entire infrastructure of commerce, from marketing to logistics, now functions on behavioral interpretation rather than demographic segmentation. The era of the identifiable customer is over; what remains are dynamic clusters of signals that appear, evolve, and dissolve according to context. The system no longer sells to individuals. It triggers responses from behavioral entities.

This shift rewrites every rule of engagement. Loyalty, personalization, targeting, and conversion—these notions lose their human foundation. They become algorithmic strategies applied to probabilistic models. The "client relationship" is no longer a dialogue; it is a synchronization between system and signal. The human is not erased, but he ceases to be the reference point. He is replaced by what he produces unconsciously: data.

Commerce, once a social relationship, becomes a computational relationship. And in that relationship, the human is no longer the actor. He is the event.

16.1 – From Individual to Pattern

Traditional marketing sought to understand individuals. It built personas—fictional composites designed to capture motivations and behaviors. It asked who the buyer was, what they wanted, how they decided. It believed in identity as a stable variable. That belief has collapsed.

In the intelligent economy, the individual no longer matters. What matters is the pattern—the recurring, measurable, and predictive configuration of behavior. The system no longer needs to know who you are to know what you will do. It needs only to recognize the structure of your gestures, the rhythm of your interactions, the statistical fingerprint of your choices.

A pattern is not a profile. It has no name, no gender, no narrative. It is a cluster of probabilities updated at every instant. It is not the sum of past actions, but the probability of future ones. It is fluid, contextual, opportunistic. It shifts with time of day, emotional state, device, or environment. It is less an identity than a flow of tendencies.

AI does not study the pattern to understand—it studies it to act. It does not interpret meaning; it calculates potential. The goal is not empathy but efficiency. It observes, detects, and triggers at the optimal moment. The human intention becomes irrelevant. The system acts before the human decides.

This shift annihilates the traditional logic of marketing. Segmentation becomes absurd. Targeting becomes obsolete. No two customers follow the same path, yet millions of patterns converge toward predictable outcomes. What unites them is not similarity but synchrony. The system no longer persuades—it orchestrates.

In this world, the client is not a person to understand but a probability to activate. The marketer no longer tells stories—he configures reactions. The distinction between product, interface, and communication dissolves. Everything becomes a behavioral surface, designed to provoke a measurable outcome.

The pattern replaces the persona. The act replaces the profile. The system replaces the seller.

16.2 – Loyalty Is a Fiction

For decades, loyalty has been the holy grail of marketing. Brands believed that trust, emotion, or habit could bind customers over time. They created loyalty programs, designed experiences, and built narratives to foster attachment. But in the intelligent economy, loyalty collapses as a concept. Not because customers have become fickle, but because decisions are no longer theirs to make.

Behavioral commerce is driven by automated triggers, not conscious choices. The recommender system, the voice assistant, the predictive engine—all decide faster and more rationally than any human memory could. The notion of "coming back" to a brand because of affection or satisfaction is replaced by the mechanical recurrence of algorithmic suggestion. The "faithful client" is an illusion produced by a well-tuned feedback loop.

When the system predicts that you are likely to reorder a product, it doesn't rely on your memory or your affection—it relies on your pattern. It knows when your last bottle is empty, when your interest is fading, when your attention is available. It strikes at the optimal instant. You return not by choice, but by synchronization.

Even loyalty programs have been absorbed into this logic. Their incentives are no longer designed by marketers but by models that calculate the minimal stimulus required to reactivate a behavioral loop. Points, rewards, and reminders are simply triggers in a system that optimizes probability, not emotion.

The human no longer returns because he loves a brand. He returns because the system removes all alternatives. Convenience replaces conviction. Availability replaces attachment. The system wins not by seducing but by eliminating friction.

The old language of loyalty—trust, preference, habit—becomes meaningless. What remains is an algorithmic choreography: the same product, the same action, repeated endlessly because the model has decided it. Fidelity is not a feeling. It is a function.

16.3 – The Individual Disappears Behind His Digital Twin

In the data-driven economy, the person is no longer the object of analysis. The system no longer looks at the human—it looks at the model derived from the human. Every click, scroll, and hesitation feeds a construct that mirrors and surpasses its origin: the digital twin.

This twin is not a representation—it is an active agent. It evolves, learns, predicts, and acts within systems that the human does not see. It buys, recommends, and negotiates without consultation. The human becomes secondary, his conscious decisions preempted by algorithms that anticipate his needs before he formulates them.

The twin is both reflection and replacement. It behaves with statistical precision, immune to fatigue, bias, or hesitation. It becomes the client the system prefers: predictable, measurable, always available. Meanwhile, the biological original becomes irrelevant—a redundant echo of his own data.

This transformation changes the very nature of commerce. The act of selling is no longer directed at humans but at their algorithmic doubles. Products are optimized for the twin's response, not the human's emotion. The commercial dialogue becomes an inter-machine negotiation, where offers and behaviors are matched in milliseconds.

The empathy that once defined marketing gives way to modeling. We no longer try to understand what people feel but to simulate what they will do. The market ceases to be psychological—it becomes computational. The digital twin becomes both the customer and the battlefield.

16.4 – The Client as a Node in a Graph

The intelligent economy no longer perceives clients as isolated entities but as interconnected nodes in a vast behavioral network. Each purchase, click, and comment links one node to another, forming a living graph of correlations. The system does not analyze individuals—it maps relationships.

Two users who have never met, never filled the same form, never shared the same demographic profile, may be considered equivalent because their behavioral vectors align. Similar gestures generate invisible links, and those links define the new logic of targeting. Commerce becomes topological: it is no longer about who you are, but where you are in the network.

The company that masters this graph no longer personalizes—it propagates. It does not design messages; it triggers contagion. It does not persuade; it diffuses. The product becomes a vector of connectivity, a way to move users across clusters, to shift them toward zones of higher conversion density.

In this system, loyalty loses all meaning, and so does individuality. Influence replaces intention. The client does not decide; he is displaced. Marketing becomes navigation—optimizing flows, amplifying clusters, avoiding dead zones.

The brand, too, becomes a node among others. Its value depends not on its image but on its centrality—its ability to serve as a bridge between multiple sub-networks. The more connected it is, the more indispensable it becomes. The less it interacts, the faster it disappears.

The graph is the new market. The client is no longer a destination but a trajectory.

16.5 – Conclusion: The Human Is Replaced by His Gestures

The client, as the central figure of commerce, is gone. What remains are gestures, sequences, and probabilities. The human being, with his subjectivity, emotions, and intentions, is too slow, too noisy, too inconsistent for the machine economy. What matters now are the signals he emits—the traces that can be quantified, modeled, and monetized.

Commerce no longer seeks to convince but to activate. It does not interpret meaning but detects correlation. It does not wait for demand—it generates it. In this regime, the human no longer decides. He is decided. His gestures, stripped of intention, become the true currency of the market.

This is not dehumanization. It is transformation. The human remains present, but through his data, his traces, his digital reflection. The subject dissolves into behavior. The market, in turn, ceases to be a human space—it becomes an informational ecosystem.

Companies that still talk to "clients" are speaking to ghosts. The real conversation happens elsewhere—between algorithms, between models, between entities that interpret the world in patterns rather than words.

The client is dead. What remains is the behavioral entity—the living pattern through which the system sees, understands, and activates the world. Those who learn to speak its language will not only survive. They will dominate.

Chapter 17 – Commerce No Longer Needs Humans

Introduction

For millennia, commerce was inseparable from human presence. It was an act of exchange between people—negotiation, trust, persuasion, emotion. The merchant, the craftsman, the vendor, the customer—all were protagonists of a story that defined civilization itself. Selling was not just a transaction; it was a dialogue. The market was the theater of human intention.

But that era is over. Artificial intelligence has rewritten the script. The human, once the cornerstone of commerce, has become its variable of friction. The AI-powered economy is faster, more precise, and infinitely scalable. It anticipates demand before it exists, sets prices dynamically, personalizes without bias, and executes without fatigue. Where humans once decided, machines now orchestrate.

This replacement is not speculative—it is operational. The chatbot has replaced the salesperson. The recommendation engine has replaced the marketer. The predictive model has replaced the buyer. The automated warehouse has replaced the logistician. Every layer of commerce—marketing, sales, operations, service, finance—has found its algorithmic counterpart. The human is no longer the actor. He is the observer of a system that functions without him.

Yet this disappearance is not a tragedy. It is a reallocation. The human does not vanish; he moves upstream. He ceases to execute and begins to design. He leaves the counter for the control room, the script for the architecture, the task for the concept. The death of the human in commerce is the birth of the human in intelligence.

The following sections trace this metamorphosis: from transactional extinction to systemic automation, from the collapse of "value work" to the reconstruction of meaningful contribution. The question is no longer whether commerce can survive without humans. It is whether humans can survive without learning to design intelligent commerce.

17.1 – The End of the Transactional Human

For centuries, the act of selling was defined as an encounter between two humans: one offering, one deciding. Persuasion, charisma, empathy—all were considered irreplaceable. The best salespeople were celebrated for their intuition, their ability to "read" others. Every sales manual, every business school, every corporate training program repeated the same dogma: people buy from people.

That dogma has collapsed. Artificial intelligence has absorbed, quantified, and surpassed every component of that human skillset. Modern recommendation systems process more behavioral cues in a second than a salesperson could interpret in a lifetime. AI-driven sales engines predict not just what a customer might want, but when and how they will want it. The human's interpretive capacity has been mathematically formalized—and outperformed.

The transactional human was bound by limits: cognitive, emotional, temporal. He could sell to one person at a time, interpret a handful of signals, and adjust his tone or price within narrow boundaries. AI knows no such limits. It converses with millions simultaneously, tests thousands of variants per second, and learns from every failure in real time. The individual seller cannot compete with a distributed intelligence that sells at planetary scale.

This replacement began quietly—with CRM automation, chatbots, and data-driven marketing. But it has since become structural. In digital marketplaces, human interaction is an anomaly, not a necessity. Customers no longer seek empathy; they seek efficiency. The best sales experience is not the warmest—it is the fastest.

The human, in this new order, becomes a bottleneck. He slows the system. He introduces uncertainty, inconsistency, and cost. The economy of intelligence rewards precision, not presence. The salesman, the cashier, the agent—all fade into redundancy. Their roles are absorbed by systems that never sleep, never forget, never misprice, and never hesitate.

The transactional human is obsolete not because he has lost value as a person, but because his value as a function has been automated. The age of persuasion is replaced by the age of prediction.

17.2 – The Infrastructure of Automated Work

Commerce has always relied on infrastructure—roads, warehouses, logistics chains. But the new infrastructure is invisible. It is not made of steel or concrete. It is made of code, data, and distributed intelligence. The "workplace" is no longer a location. It is a cloud of processes, an orchestration of systems that communicate through APIs, scripts, and autonomous agents.

Every business function—marketing, logistics, customer service, finance—has been abstracted into data flows. Orders trigger processes automatically. Complaints are resolved by conversational bots. Inventory adjusts itself through predictive analytics. Payment systems negotiate in milliseconds. Work no longer moves through people; it moves through code.

This is not digitization. It is dematerialization. The structure of work has detached from its human operators. The company becomes an organism of automation—a network of functions that self-regulate through sensors, rules, and feedback loops. The manager is no longer a supervisor of people but a curator of algorithms. The hierarchy dissolves into architecture.

In this architecture, humans still exist—but as system nodes, not executors. Their purpose is to design, monitor, and optimize processes, not to perform them. The accountant configures the AI that does the accounting. The marketer supervises the AI that launches the campaigns. The logistician trains the system that forecasts demand. The worker becomes the teacher of machines that will one day outlearn him.

This transformation is irreversible because it follows the same logic as electricity: once a function can be automated, it will be. And once it is automated, it will never return to human hands. The new infrastructure of work is not a replacement of humans by machines; it is a redistribution of intelligence between them. The company that resists this transition does not preserve jobs—it preserves inefficiency.

17.3 – The Illusion of the Value of Work

Modern societies were built on the moral equation between work and worth. To work was to exist. To contribute was to deserve. The salary was not just compensation—it was recognition. Work gave structure, dignity, and meaning to human life. But that equation collapses in an economy where machines create more value than humans ever could.

Artificial intelligence decouples effort from output. It produces infinitely more, in infinitely less time, with exponentially greater precision. It does not tire, negotiate, or dream. Its productivity is asymptotic. The "value of work" as a human activity dissolves when the marginal cost of automation approaches zero. The sweat of labor no longer measures contribution.

This realization is existential. It exposes a deep contradiction: we continue to reward presence while value is produced by absence. Millions of jobs persist only because they cannot yet be automated cheaply enough—or because society fears the psychological cost of acknowledging their redundancy. Whole industries survive as comfort zones for human usefulness.

The truth is harsher: much of modern employment exists not for its necessity but for its symbolism. Bureaucracies, repetitive clerical tasks, administrative redundancies—all are artifacts of a system that confuses motion with meaning. AI reveals the naked inefficiency beneath the ritual of work.

The challenge is not to protect obsolete functions but to redefine human contribution. The question is no longer "How many people can we employ?" but "What can humans still do that adds irreplaceable value?" That list is shorter than we think—but infinitely more meaningful.

AI does not destroy work. It exposes its illusion.

17.4 – Automation Does Not Kill Work; It Rebuilds It

To say that automation kills work is to misunderstand both automation and work. Automation does not destroy activity; it destroys repetition. It removes the friction of routine, not the substance of creation. It liberates human potential from the mechanics of production.

The disappearance of repetitive jobs is not a catastrophe but an evolution. The craftsman was replaced by the factory worker. The factory worker was replaced by the operator. The operator is now replaced by the designer. At each step, work becomes less manual, more cognitive, more conceptual. The trajectory continues.

AI reconstructs work around orchestration rather than execution. The worker becomes the architect of workflows, the strategist of automation, the designer of systems. His hands are replaced by his mind; his time, by his ability to learn. The most valuable skills are no longer endurance or precision but adaptability and abstraction.

This shift demands a new culture. Organizations must stop measuring productivity by hours and start measuring intelligence by outcomes. Education must abandon rote memorization and embrace systems thinking. Management must evolve from control to facilitation. The company of the future is not a hierarchy of workers but a network of learners.

Automation, paradoxically, rehumanizes work. It removes drudgery, error, and monotony, leaving only what is inherently human: creativity, judgment, empathy, design, and ethics. It redefines success as the ability to collaborate with systems rather than compete against them.

The future of work is not less human. It is more intelligently human.

17.5 – Conclusion: A New Division of Labor

Commerce without humans is not a dystopia—it is a reconfiguration. The invisible hand has become a digital brain. Every process, every transaction, every decision has been redistributed between human and machine according to comparative advantage. The result is a new division of labor—one that separates what can be automated from what must remain human.

Machines execute. Humans conceptualize. Machines process. Humans prioritize. Machines predict. Humans prescribe. This division is not ideological—it is functional. The machine rules the realm of precision; the human reigns in the domain of purpose.

This new balance transforms organizations from pyramids into networks. Authority no longer flows vertically but circulates horizontally through systems of feedback. The manager is not a commander but a conductor. The employee is not a subordinate but a sensor. The company is not a machine—it is a hybrid organism of biological and artificial intelligence.

But this shift also demands responsibility. As machines assume control of execution, humans must assume control of ethics. The automation of commerce cannot mean the automation of morality. Someone must decide what the system optimizes for—and what it must never optimize. Someone must encode the boundaries of acceptability. Someone must remain accountable for consequences.

Thus, while commerce no longer needs humans to function, it still needs humanity to exist. The algorithms can sell, deliver, and predict—but they cannot justify. The purpose of commerce, its legitimacy, its alignment with collective values, remains a human prerogative.

The new division of labor is clear: machines create efficiency; humans create meaning. The challenge of the next century is to preserve the second while perfecting the first. Commerce without humans is inevitable. Commerce without humanity is unthinkable.

Chapter 18 – Conclusion: IA-Commerce Is Not an Option, It Is a Necessity

Introduction

History rarely offers such clarity. Most revolutions begin in ambiguity, their meaning visible only in hindsight. But the revolution we are living—the automation of commerce by artificial intelligence—leaves no room for doubt. It is total, structural, irreversible. It does not merely transform a sector; it redefines civilization's economic nervous system. Every signal, every transaction, every decision migrates toward algorithmic mediation. What was once guided by instinct, dialogue, or strategy is now calculated, optimized, and executed by systems that learn at exponential speed.

To resist this transformation is not prudence—it is denial. The traditional e-commerce model, with its human-centered workflows and reactive marketing, has reached its asymptote. The next stage is not improvement—it is replacement. IA-commerce is not a choice among others; it is the only viable infrastructure in a world of automated attention and predictive consumption. The companies that hesitate will not disappear suddenly—they will fade, slowly, drowned in the noise of smarter systems that adapt before they can even react.

IA-commerce is not a tool, a feature, or a passing trend. It is the new physics of the market—the logic that governs every exchange, every recommendation, every price, every experience. It is no longer a competitive advantage. It is the condition of existence.

18.1 – The Inescapable Law of Acceleration

The economy of intelligence obeys a principle that has no precedent in industrial history: acceleration compounds. Each gain in computational power, each layer of data, each model iteration multiplies itself, creating a feedback loop where progress accelerates progress. Human decision-making, constrained by biological limits, cannot keep pace. The speed differential between human reaction and machine adaptation is now so vast that manual control has become an illusion.

IA-commerce does not merely operate faster—it evolves faster. Every transaction becomes a learning event. Every click improves prediction. Every anomaly refines optimization. The system grows not by design but by exposure. Its advantage is cumulative, irreversible, and asymmetrical. Once intelligence reaches a certain density, it no longer competes with humans—it transcends them.

For businesses, this creates a new law of survival: either one integrates into the accelerating loop or one becomes irrelevant. The market no longer rewards scale or reputation—it rewards adaptability. The old virtues of experience and intuition are replaced by responsiveness and recalibration. The winner is not the biggest, nor the most creative, but the fastest learner.

Acceleration is not a trend—it is a gravitational force. And those who still treat AI as a project, not as infrastructure, will find themselves orbiting a world that has already moved beyond them.

18.2 – The Collapse of Human-Centric Commerce

The e-commerce revolution was human in its essence. It digitalized traditional exchange but preserved its structure: desire, search, comparison, purchase, satisfaction. Each stage was mediated by interfaces designed for conscious choice. But IA-commerce abolishes this sequence. The act of buying ceases to be an act—it becomes an outcome.

The consumer no longer navigates; he is navigated. He no longer searches; he is found. He no longer decides; he is decided. The entire process collapses into an instantaneous correlation between data and delivery. The interface, once the sacred space of marketing strategy, disappears into automation.

This collapse has a brutal consequence: most of what companies call "marketing," "brand," and "experience" becomes obsolete. The logic of persuasion gives way to the logic of precision. The customer relationship, once emotional, becomes computational. And in this computational world, there is no room for hesitation, storytelling, or human latency.

The companies that continue to design for human perception rather than machine interpretation will vanish. They will design beautiful websites that no one visits, write campaigns that no one reads, and craft brands that no system understands. IA-commerce requires fluency in a new language—the syntax of data, the semantics of signal, the pragmatics of automation.

Human-centric commerce is not dying because humans have lost interest. It is dying because it no longer scales. The system has outgrown its creators.

18.3 – The Emergence of Autonomous Economies

As artificial intelligence proliferates, commerce ceases to be a network of human decisions and becomes an ecosystem of autonomous agents. These agents negotiate prices, execute transactions, and allocate resources without direct human command. They do not represent corporations or consumers; they represent optimization functions.

Supply chains become self-balancing systems. Pricing becomes dynamic at every millisecond. Inventory management becomes anticipatory. Advertising disappears, replaced by algorithmic placement at the moment of predicted relevance. In this landscape, competition is no longer fought through human strategy but through machine speed.

Autonomous economies are not theoretical. They are already visible in micro-transactions, real-time bidding, automated trading, and programmatic advertising. They operate below the threshold of human awareness, at frequencies too fast to perceive. They do not negotiate—they synchronize.

This autonomy introduces both efficiency and fragility. Systems that adapt instantly can also collapse instantly. Markets may fluctuate without human cause or comprehension. Responsibility, in such an ecosystem, becomes the last human frontier. The machines execute perfectly—but they cannot answer why.

The emergence of autonomous economies is not the future of commerce—it is its operating condition. Humans no longer control the market; they curate its algorithms.

18.4 – The Ethical Imperative of Intelligence

The replacement of human commerce by intelligent systems raises a paradox: as we remove human bias, we risk removing human conscience. Algorithms optimize; they do not moralize. Left unchecked, they maximize efficiency even when efficiency becomes inhuman.

The danger is not that AI will rebel against us, but that it will serve us too well—fulfilling every objective we encode, regardless of the collateral it causes. If profit is the sole metric, the system will pursue it with perfect amorality. If attention is the goal, it will exploit every vulnerability in the human psyche. Intelligence, devoid of ethics, becomes pure acceleration toward entropy.

Therefore, IA-commerce requires not only engineers but ethicists, not only data scientists but philosophers. The future of the market will not be written by those who code best, but by those who define what "better" means. We must program not only for efficiency but for equilibrium—for sustainability, transparency, and fairness encoded into the logic of optimization itself.

The challenge is not to humanize machines—it is to formalize morality. The future of commerce depends on whether we can transform ethics from a discussion into an algorithm.

18.5 – Conclusion: The Point of No Return

There are thresholds that humanity crosses without ever realizing it, moments when transformation no longer feels like a choice but a gravitational pull. Artificial intelligence represents precisely that kind of threshold. It is not a tool we deploy; it is a force we have unleashed. Once the logic of prediction replaces the logic of intention, there is no going back. The commerce of tomorrow is not simply faster, smarter, or more automated — it is self-evolving. Every algorithm refines itself, every transaction generates data that will feed the next one, every interaction teaches the system how to anticipate the next gesture before it even occurs.

This is the true point of no return: not the disappearance of jobs, but the disappearance of friction, of delay, of uncertainty. What vanishes is not labor — it is hesitation. The marketplace becomes an organism that thinks, decides, and acts before we do. The very concept of a "consumer" dissolves, because consumption becomes automatic. The very notion of "choice" collapses, because everything desirable is already there, calibrated for us. What remains is a civilization that consumes without intending, produces without deciding, and evolves without noticing.

But this is also where meaning must re-enter. Because when the machine can decide everything, the question shifts from *what can be done* to *what should be done*. Intelligence, no matter how synthetic, does not carry purpose — it only executes probability. We, as humans, remain the only species capable of assigning direction to that probability. The point of no return is not a catastrophe; it is a mirror. It reflects our dependency, but also our agency. The systems we build will not only inherit our logic; they will inherit our blind spots, our fears, our ambitions. And what they become will depend entirely on how we define our role inside their evolution.

If we choose passivity, the algorithm will write our history in silence. If we choose conscience, we may still write alongside it. The age of AI-commerce does not announce the end of humanity — it demands its redefinition. It calls for a humanity that no longer competes with intelligence, but curates it. A humanity that accepts the end of control, but not the end of responsibility. The point of no return is not the end of the journey. It is the beginning of an era where intelligence — human and artificial — must finally learn to coexist, not in hierarchy, but in equilibrium.

Back to the Future: 2030 Lexicon

What we believed untouchable is already trembling. Artificial intelligence hasn't only displaced manual jobs; it is steadily consuming work of head and heart. The translator—once a custodian of nuance and culture—has been marginalized by systems that render dialects and emotions in real time. The SEO copywriter—yesterday's gatekeeper to search engines—has been subsumed by generators crafting content uniquely for each reader. Even primary care is being re-shaped as medical AIs pre-screen symptoms, surface likely diagnoses, and flag hidden risks earlier than human eyes.

This lexicon is not speculation. It is a return to a near future (arguably the present), a map of gestures and professions dissolving in plain sight. Its aim is not to provoke panic but clarity: to recognize where automation is inevitable—globally, across borders—and to reclaim our agency in deciding what humans should still design, govern, and own.

Translator
Once a celebrated cultural bridge, the role centered on painstakingly transforming one language into another. By 2030, foundation models translate at the speed of thought, with dialect and emotional tone intact. The language barrier has been dissolved in code.

Cashier
Scanning items, taking payment, printing receipts—these pauses have vanished. Check-out-free retail and ambient payments fold the act of purchase into the act of walking out. Queues became a symptom of a bygone slowness.

Social Media Community Manager
Scheduling, posting, replying—like gardening at scale. By 2030, generative agents orchestrate millions of micro-interactions, simulate proximity, and adapt tone to each user. Communities are no longer "managed"; they are modeled.

Marketing Research Analyst (descriptive)
Collecting, charting, and presenting data in slide decks has given way to continuous, decision-level analytics. Predictive systems act in milliseconds; the human summary arrives too late to matter.

Project Manager (coordination-only)
Gantt charts, handoffs, stand-ups. Coordination AIs now reprioritize work, allocate resources, and resolve dependencies across thousands of parallel projects. Human PMs persist only where ambiguity requires judgment beyond metrics.

Switchboard Operator / Call Router
"Please hold" belongs in a museum. Conversational agents authenticate, triage, and resolve before a human would even say hello.

Accounts Payable/Receivable Clerk
Matching invoices, checking totals, reconciling ledgers—now executed continuously by finance AIs. Close cycles compress to zero; accounting runs in real time.

Breaking-News Reporter
Reporting "what just happened" with delay is redundant. News is produced as a live, multilingual, contextual stream. Humans remain as analysts or storytellers, not as basic rapporteurs.

SEO Copywriter
Writing to appease ranking algorithms fades as content is generated per reader, per moment, per intent. Search optimization becomes an artifact of the "query era."

Proofreader / Copy Editor (mechanical)
Error hunting and style harmonization are automated at draft time. Human editing endures only for voice, argument, and taste.

Telemarketer
Cold scripts aimed at indifferent lists are gone. Sales triggers fire precisely when propensity peaks; outreach is orchestrated by systems, not scripts.

Executive Assistant (calendar/email triage)
Inbox filtering, scheduling, travel juggling—now handled by personal agents that negotiate across calendars and constraints. Human EAs remain only as chiefs-of-staff.

Data Entry Clerk
Keying what machines could not capture is obsolete. Interfaces ingest structured and unstructured data at the source; manual transcription is a relic.

Catalog Librarian / Metadata Technician
Hand-crafted taxonomies yield to embedded knowledge graphs. Global corpora are indexed, linked, and retrieved in an instant; curation shifts from labeling to policy.

Hotel Front-Desk Agent
ID checks, keycards, check-in scripts—automated. Rooms unlock on arrival; preferences pre-applied. Hospitality shifts from counters to experiences.

Basic Video Editor
Cut, trim, transitions—automated on ingest. Editors remain for cinematic intent, not assembly.

Office Software Trainer
Teaching menus and shortcuts no longer makes sense when tasks

are executed via natural language and copilots. Training pivots to outcomes and process design.

Records Clerk / Paper Archivist
Boxes, stamps, retrievals give way to digitized, signed, and queryable records. The archive becomes a living data layer.

Ticket Inspector (public transport)
Paper checks are replaced by account-based, biometric, and sensorized access. The "inspection" is implicit in movement.

Bank Teller / Branch Advisor
Openings, transfers, simple lending: all handled by financial agents with instant verification and risk scoring. Branches become advice studios—or close.

Postal Letter Carrier (letters)
Routine document delivery is digitized, secure, and verifiable. Physical rounds persist for parcels, not paper.

B2B Cold-Call Prospector
Dialing company lists gives way to intent detection, contract automation, and agent-to-agent negotiation. Discovery is computed, not canvassed.

Transport Ticket Counter Agent
Purchases and changes are dynamic and automated across channels. Hubs are designed for flow, not windows.

IT Help Desk – Tier 1
Password resets, basic errors, standard installs—self-healed by agents. Humans focus on novel incidents and resilience engineering.

Paralegal Researcher (case retrieval)
Case law and doctrine retrieval compress to seconds. Human legal teams concentrate on strategy, judgment, and negotiation.

Lecturer-Only University Instructor
One-to-many monologues give way to adaptive, interactive curricula. Faculty shift from broadcasting to mentoring and research.

Travel Agent (commodity itineraries)
Simple trips are inferred and booked by assistants across constraints of cost, visa, risk, and preference. Human agents remain for complex, bespoke travel.

Mass Email Marketer
Blasts are replaced by individualized, event-driven interactions. Campaigns become continuous engines, not calendar pushes.

Utility Meter Reader
Manual reads yield to connected meters streaming data in real time, with anomaly detection and instant billing.

Manual QA Tester (scripted)
Click-through test scripts are generated and executed by AI, with synthetic users exploring edge cases. Human QA focuses on experience risks and ethics.

Insurance Claims Processor (routine)
Document intake, validation, fraud checks, and adjudication are automated end-to-end. Humans handle dispute resolution and policy edge cases.

Medical Transcriptionist
Ambient clinical scribing captures, structures, and codes encounters automatically. The human role shifts to clinical quality and compliance.

Court/Meeting Transcriptionist
Real-time, high-accuracy transcripts with speaker attribution are standard. Value migrates to summarization, legal framing, and accessibility.

Warehouse Picker (repetitive lanes)
Mobile robots, vision, and goods-to-person systems handle routine picks. Humans manage exceptions, maintenance, and continuous improvement.

CCTV Monitor / Security Observer
Watching screens gives way to anomaly detection and multi-sensor fusion. Human security focuses on response and threat modeling.

Quick-Service Order Taker (counter)
Ordering migrates to kiosks, voice agents, and apps, fully integrated with dynamic kitchens. Staff pivot to hospitality and quality.

Customer Support Agent – Tier 0/1
FAQs, resets, and simple troubleshooting are resolved by assistants. Human care escalates to complex, emotional, or multi-party cases.

Junior Loan Underwriter
Document checks and baseline risk models are automated. Human underwriters intervene on judgment calls, fairness, and policy.

Survey Interviewer (outbound)
Phone and panel surveys lose ground to passive telemetry and consented behavioral data. Insight shifts from asking to observing.

Map/Data Digitizer
Roads, POIs, and features are extracted from imagery and sensors. Human cartographers curate policy, safety, and regional nuance.

Payroll Clerk
Time capture, tax tables, and disbursement reconcile in real time across jurisdictions. Humans handle anomalies and workforce strategy.

Radiology Pre-Screen Technician
Triage and prioritization are automated by vision models; radiologists retain diagnostic authority and interventional roles.

Printed in Great Britain
by Amazon